THE STUDENT EARTH SCIENTIST
EXPLORES WEATHER

THE STUDENT EARTH SCIENTIST EXPLORES WEATHER

By

Constantine Constant

Illustrated by

Nancy Lou Gahan

RICHARDS ROSEN PRESS, INC.
New York, New York 10010

Published in 1975 by Richards Rosen Press, Inc.
29 East 21st Street, New York, N.Y. 10010

Copyright 1975 by Constantine Constant

First Edition

Library of Congress Cataloging in Publication Data

Constant, Constantine.
    The student earth scientist explores weather.

    Bibliography: p.
    1. Weather.   I.   Gahan, Nancy Lou, illus.
II. Title.
QC981.C715   551.6   74-13746
ISBN 0-8239-0303-6

Manufactured in the United States of America

About the Author

Constantine Constant (known as Gus to his friends) has to his credit an impressive array of publications in Earth Science, but he is a good deal more than a teacher and writer. During World War II he served as a weatherman for the United States Navy, and in the early 1950's he also was on the staff of the United States Geological Survey, a division of the Department of the Interior.

Born in Pawtucket, Rhode Island, he was educated at Hofstra University, New York University, and Hunter College, all in Greater New York, and he holds the degrees of bachelor and master. His teaching experience in various fields of science ranges from elementary school through junior and senior high school, to college. He is currently a teacher of Earth Science at Forest Hills High School, New York.

Mr. Constant's publications include *Energy Changes in the Atmosphere and Hydrosphere, Matter and Life in Space, Review Text in Earth Science*, and an *Earth Science* workbook. He has prepared experimental and regular science curricula for the New York City Public Schools, which are used all over the United States. Among his many scientific articles, a number have been translated into the French and German languages and have been published in Switzerland.

Contents

THE STUDENT EARTH SCIENTIST
EXPLORES WEATHER

I

Clouds

> When a precipitation of vapour takes place, a multitude of
> exceedingly small drops form a cloud, mist, or fog; these
> drops, though 800 times denser than air, at first descend very
> slowly, owing to the resistance of the air . . . if the drops in
> falling enter into a stratum of air capable of imbibing vapour,
> they may be redissolved, and the clouds not descend at all . . .

These words, describing the formation of a cloud, were
written nearly 200 years ago by John Dalton, a famous
British chemist. Surprisingly, the description shows great
insight into the way clouds form in the atmosphere. The key
idea in Dalton's description of cloud formation is that
numerous tiny particles of water vapor collect (precipitate)
to form a cloud.

Other scientists of the early years also tried to explain the
phenomenon called clouds. Their descriptions of the physical
processes at work in the formation of clouds, and their
suspension in the air, are of great interest—as they were
reasonably accurate. In 1749 Benjamin Franklin, the American statesman and scientist, for example, described how
differences in the heating of the land result in heated parcels
of air rising and cooler parcels above the ground descending.
He went on to describe the formation of thunderclouds and

their accompanying lightning and thunder as a result of these air movements. Only a few years later, in 1752, Franklin discovered the electrical nature of lightning.

Other examples include the proposal by the German scientist Johann Heinrich Lambert, in 1765, that "the air will be expanded only where the heat has increased." He further stated that the expanding air will upset the equilibrium of the upper air and that this disturbance results in circulation of the air. In 1850 the American meteorologist James Espy stated that the suspension of clouds depends upon upward-moving columns of air in the atmosphere.

Modern scientists, having more knowledge and advanced skills and methods of probing clouds, have made important discoveries about clouds, including how they form, what they are made of, and why they have different shapes. As you read through this chapter, see if you can identify processes related to cloud formation that are generally similar to those described by Dalton, Franklin, Lambert, and Espy.

Water Vapor and Clouds

The earth's total atmosphere weighs nearly six quadrillion tons. Included in this total are gases such as nitrogen, oxygen, argon, carbon dioxide, and water vapor. Together, these gases make up over 99 percent of the total mass of the atmosphere. Of this total, water vapor accounts for about 2 percent on the average. Although nitrogen and oxygen make up the major portion of the remainder of the atmosphere, their importance in weather processes is insignificant compared to that of water vapor.

The importance of water vapor lies in its heat-absorbing properties, which cause it to act as a regulator of heat loss from the earth, and in its potential for providing the energy and moisture necessary for the formation of storms with their accompanying clouds, precipitation, and winds.

Although water vapor is always present in the air, we find that there are many hours and even days throughout the year that are cloudless and without precipitation. In regions where the humidity is very low, such as the low-latitude deserts, nearly every day of the year is sunny. For example, in the Sonora Desert in the southwestern United States and north-western Mexico, the sun shines about 75 to 90 percent of the time, depending on the season. Similar figures are common to other deserts of the world. By contrast, regions of high humidity, such as the doldrums, a region of the earth near the equator, have few cloudless days (Fig. 1). For example,

FIG. 1

in sections traversed by the Amazon River in South America, completely clear days are almost unknown.

Although desert regions are typically cloudless and tropical regions are typically sunny, we do find cloudy days occurring over the deserts occasionally, and we do find sunny days occurring in tropical regions that are usually cloudy. In fact, not only do desert regions have some cloudy days, but at times heavy rainfalls also occur over small areas of most deserts.

It is important to note that the air over desert regions, although extremely dry, contains large amounts of moisture, which under the proper conditions can be triggered to form other condensation forms. This is evident in desert regions where dew forms on the ground and other surfaces during relatively cold nights. It is not unusual for desert temperatures to drop to near freezing, or below, at night. Some desert dwellers take advantage of this phenomenon by piling up masses of boulders upon which dew collects and forms drops that drip off the rocks and collect in pools. In this way these people supply themselves with large amounts of fresh water. The two conditions that make it possible for the desert dwellers to collect water from the air for their use are also important in the condensation of water vapor in the air, which results in the formation of clouds. These conditions are:

(1) cooling of the air to the dew point, and
(2) availability of objects upon which water vapor can collect.

Clouds From the Sea

We have seen that the largest possible source of water vapor in the atmosphere is the ocean. The movement of water from the ocean, although unseen, is a continuous process. It is a process that involves the changing of a liquid (sea water) into a gas. This process is evaporation. You may recall that energy is required to produce changes of state in matter. The change in state from liquid to gas is quite obvious when we watch water boiling over a fire. Before long, a pot of boiling water will disappear — ask any housewife. Evaporation is rapid during boiling, since the heat energy absorbed by the water causes a tremendous increase in the kinetic energy of the water molecules. The increased motion of the water molecules causes the water molecules to move farther apart. At the surface of the liquid, water molecules break loose from the liquid and move into the air. By contrast, movement within cooler water is much slower — yet evaporation also takes place at the surface of cool water because the water molecules have kinetic energy. Although the kinetic energy is lower in cool water, it is adequate to cause water molecules to break loose from the surface. Thus, although the ocean waters are relatively cold — ranging from about 28° F. in arctic waters to about 86° F. in equatorial waters — evaporation of the ocean waters is a continuous process (Fig. 2).

The amount of water evaporated from the ocean depends upon several factors, including temperature, vapor pressure, and the wind.

The importance of temperature in the evaporation process is obvious when we compare the time it takes for two pans of water — one heated and one unheated — to evaporate. Water in a heated pan may disappear within minutes, whereas water in an unheated pan may take hours or even days to evaporate completely.

As water molecules enter the air, they add to the moisture content or vapor pressure of the atmosphere. The more

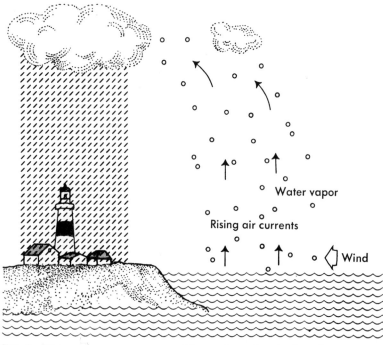

FIG. 2   *Water vapor evaporates supplying moisture for clouds and precipitation overland.*

water molecules in the air, the greater the vapor pressure. When the air becomes saturated, the vapor pressure in the air is equal to the pressure from within the liquid that is driving water molecules outward. At this time, the number of molecules leaving the liquid is balanced by the gaseous particles returning to the liquid from the air at random. Essentially then, evaporation ceases when an equilibrium point is reached. If the temperature of the air is increased, the amount of water vapor needed to saturate the air also increases; the result—more water vapor can be added to the air. Accordingly, it is from the surface of the warm tropical oceans that the greatest quantities of water enter the atmosphere.

Cloud Formation

Air masses moving onto the land from the sea are the usual sources of moisture that form the clouds above us. Much of the moisture that appears as clouds in the United States had its origin in the Atlantic and Pacific oceans and the Gulf of Mexico. Thus, when you see a cloud overhead you should be aware that the moisture in the cloud may have traveled hundreds, even thousands, of miles, from a remote part of the sea where it evaporated from the surface. And, oftentimes, the moisture-laden air traveled hundreds or thousands of miles before clouds even appeared in the sky.

The appearance of clouds in the sky ordinarily indicates that the air has cooled to its dew point. The dew point represents the temperature at which the air becomes saturated—that is, the relative humidity is 100 percent. At this point condensation begins. Condensation by cooling can readily be demonstrated on humid days by adding ice cubes to water in a drinking glass. Most people are aware that under such conditions the outside of the glass becomes wet within a few minutes. The ice-cold glass serves two purposes: first, it cools the air in contact with it; and second, it provides a surface upon which the cooled particles can collect. A similar effect takes place in the atmosphere, where dust particles provide countless surfaces upon which condensed moisture can collect and form cloud particles. The importance of dust particles as condensation centers (condensation nuclei) has been demonstrated in many laboratory experiments in which samples of air were scrubbed clean of all foreign particles. Experimenters have found that such samples of air can be cooled far below the dew point without condensation occurring. In other experiments, parcels of cleaned air, supersaturated 400 to 500 percent, failed to produce a condensate when the dew point was reached. Yet, if a small amount of particulate matter such as dust or smoke particles is added to such parcels of air, a cloud rapidly appears. The effect such particulate matter and other particles have on air is significant in cloud formation

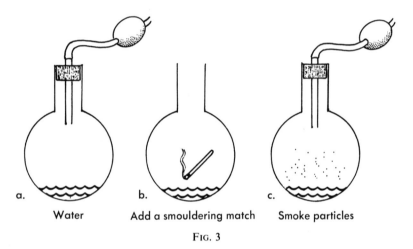

a.   Water   b.   Add a smouldering match   c.   Smoke particles

FIG. 3

because their affinity for moisture can cause condensation to occur at humidities well below 100 percent. You can see this effect by doing the following simple experiment. First: set up a flask, as shown in Fig. 3, and squeeze the bulb about three to five times. Release the clamp and look for the appearance of a cloud in the flask. Second: drop a smolder-ing match into the flask; quickly replace the rubber stopper and squeeze the bulb about three times. What do you see? Can you explain why a cloud appeared so readily? Although the smoke particles played an important part in forming a cloud in the flask, the cloud appears only when the air under pressure in the flask is released. The release of pressure causes cooling. The mechanics of cooling and its significance will be explained shortly. First let us consider the foreign particles that are of vital importance in cloud formation.

Condensation Nuclei

Scientists refer to the small foreign particles in the air as condensation nuclei because they act as centers (or seeds) upon which water vapor can collect and grow into cloud droplets. The types of condensation nuclei that are usually floating about in the air are sea salts, smoke particles from fires and volcanoes, soil particles, and meteoric dust. These particles are so numerous in the atmosphere that a cubic foot of air outside your window may contain between 25,000,000 and 100,000,000 particles. You cannot see them because they are microscopic. The diameter of these particles ranges from about 0.001 microns to about 10 microns. (A micron is one millionth of a meter, or approximately 0.00004 inches.)

Since these microscopic particles absorb water quite readily, they are also called hygroscopic (water attracting). Particles of sea salt and particles formed by combustion and lightning strokes are important hygroscopic particles found in the air. In your own experience, you have seen the absorbing ability of salts when salt shakers clog in humid weather. The salt grains, having a strong affinity for water, become "soaked," causing them to stick together. Ordinarily, adding several grains of rice to a salt shaker helps to unclog the shaker, since rice can readily absorb large amounts of water.

Hygroscopic particles produced by combustion are formed as a result of chemical changes between the air and sulfur compounds released from burning fuels such as coal and oil. The substance produced is sulfur trioxide, which has a strong affinity for water. Particles produced by lightning strokes are formed when a flash of lightning superheats the air, causing nitrogen, oxygen, and water to combine chemically and form nitrous acid, which is strongly hygroscopic. The presence of these water-absorbing chemical compounds in the air can cause the condensation of water vapor at humidities well below 100 percent.

Sea Salt and Clouds

The most important condensation nuclei are sea salts, which are much more abundant and widespread in the atmosphere. In general, salt particles are thrown into the air as part of sea spray. Thus, large amounts of salt are sprayed into the air along shores battered by breaking waves and from whitecapped waves at sea.

Since sea-spray particles appear to have an important effect on the weather and climate, scientists have done much research into the mechanism that causes these particles to be added to the air. Accordingly, researchers have directed much attention to the bubbling foam that appears when sea water is agitated.

If you have ever watched waves breaking on the shore of the ocean or a large lake, you must have seen the whitish foaming mass formed when the waves break. The foam is made up of myriads of tiny air bubbles. Similarly the treacherous white water of rapids, which canoeists respect, is made up of air bubbles produced when fast-moving water tumbles and swirls about as it rushes over numerous obstructions in its path. The same effect may occasionally be seen when a glass tumbler is filled with water—the water appears cloudy for a short while. If you looked closely you would have noticed numerous bubbles rising to the surface, and you might have seen them collecting at the surface and popping. And if you ever held a glass of freshly poured soda pop—such as a cola or root-beer drink—close to your face, you not only saw bubbles bursting, you felt them as a slight tickle on your skin. The tickling effect is caused by tiny particles of soda water being scattered about by the mini-explosions.

You may wonder what gas bubbles in water have to do with salt particles in the air. Scientists have asked the same question, and to find out have done a number of experiments. They studied bubbles in the laboratory by passing air through samples of sea water and by splashing the surface of sea-water samples with drops released from various heights. High-speed photographs showed bubbles rising from the surface of the water and then bursting. The bursting bubbles produced hundreds, even thousands, of smaller bubbles that formed a fog of particles above the water surface. These minute particles, containing sea salts, are easily lifted and carried away by moving air.

In nature, bubbles are continuously forming at the surface of the sea in waves breaking along the shore and in whitecaps that appear at sea when wind speeds exceed 7 miles per hour. In addition to the bubbles that rise into the air and burst, numerous bubbles also break at the surface of the relatively calm sea. These bubbles break when the film of water separating them from the air is disrupted. The effect is somewhat like sticking a pin in a balloon.

The bursting of these air bubbles is like the soda-water mini-explosions. By this method, numerous small particles of sea water are ejected into the atmosphere, carrying sea salts with them. These minute particles are lifted upward by air movements and are transported great distances. Since these particles come from the sea, their greatest concentrations are above the sea and in coastal areas. The billions upon billions of salt particles drifting about in the atmosphere, along with billions of tons of water evaporated from the sea and other places, will readily combine if the air temperature can be reduced close to or below the dew point. We saw earlier that air can be brought to the dew point by cooling. Air may be cooled in a number of ways, including:

(1) expansion
(2) radiation
(3) mixing with colder air
(4) contact with colder surfaces

Of these, the most important cooling process in the formation of clouds is expansion, which results when parcels of air move upward in the atmosphere (Fig. 4). As a parcel of air rises, it moves into regions of thinner air. Accordingly, the surrounding air pressure becomes progressively lower, and the parcel of air expands under its own pressure. The effect of expansion is cooling within the rising parcel of air. This effect was demonstrated earlier (see Fig. 3) when air was compressed in a flask and then released. The compressed air may be compared to air near the earth's surface that is compressed by the huge mass of overlying air. When the air in the flask was suddenly released, the pressure within the flask dropped sharply. In effect, rapid expansion occurred. In the atmosphere, the same effect is accomplished when air is lifted into regions of lower pressure. In this case, however, expansion is relatively slow since the pressure acting upon the parcel is reduced slowly. In both instances

cooling takes place because expansion constitutes work, and
to do work energy is expended. Since the energy used up is
heat energy, cooling occurs.

In a rising parcel of "dry air" (air in which the relative
humidity is less than 100 percent)
the air cools at a rate of 5.5° F.
for every 1,000 feet of altitude.
This is known as the dry adiabatic rate. (Adiabatic denotes a
temperature change within the
parcel of air itself.) By comparison, the usual decrease in temperature with increasing altitude
(the normal lapse rate) is about
3.3° F. per 1,000 feet.

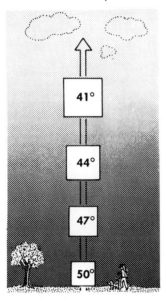

Thinner air—Lower pressure

41°

44°

47°

50°

F<small>IG</small>. 4

As air rises, then, it expands
and cools at a rate of 5.5% F. per
1,000 feet. Thus, a sample of air
with a temperature of 60° F. at
the surface, when lifted to a height
of 2,000 feet, should be 11 degrees cooler, or 49° F. Accordingly, as the parcel continues to
rise it continues to cool. Eventually, the combination of cooling
and the presence of condensation
nuclei causes the water vapor in the air to collect into cloud
droplets.

The importance of condensation nuclei in the formation
of clouds is in their ability to collect water droplets and keep
them from evaporating back into the air. You recall how
higher saturations are needed to cause condensation in
cleaned air. When droplets are produced under such condi-

tions they have a strong tendency to evaporate; condensation nuclei retard them.

Researchers have noticed that the size and type of condensation nuclei play an important part in cloud formation. They have found that large, strongly hygroscopic particles are most effective in producing cloud droplets. They have also found that cloud growth usually begins with condensation of water vapor on large nuclei. As a cloud becomes increasingly saturated, however, condensation begins on the smaller droplets; then the smaller droplets grow more rapidly than the large ones. Thus, the smaller droplets also play an important role in the development of clouds. Since all cloud particles are extremely small, clouds are easily held aloft and transported by air movements as slow as about 9 feet per minute.

Cloud Types

To the casual observer clouds may appear to have so many forms that it is difficult to place them in classes. Actually, most clouds fit into three categories (Fig. 5) — cumulus (puffy clouds), stratiform or stratus (flat clouds), and cirrus (ice clouds).

The outward appearances of cumulus and stratus clearly indicate the types of air movements taking place in the atmosphere. Thus, these shapes tell scientists much about the physical processes at work in the atmosphere. The most common cumuliform clouds are probably cumulus clouds, which often appear as white, puffed-up masses scattered across the sky. Their appearance indicates the presence of invisible columns of relatively warm, moist air that are swirling upward rapidly, with the air movement being largely vertical. The force that drives the air upward is ordinarily

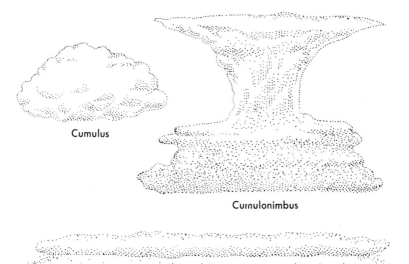

Cumulus

Cumulonimbus

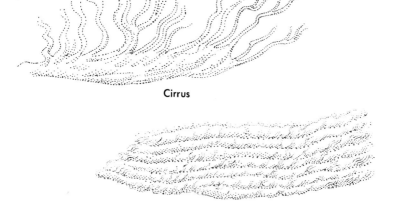

Strato cumulus

Cirrus

Cirrocumulus

FIG. 5 *Cloud Types*

caused by the unequal heating of the land. In addition, cumuliform clouds are also produced when masses of warm moist air are forced upward by advancing fronts, or by land barriers in the path of the moving masses.

The bases of cumulus clouds indicate the point at which the dew point was reached. In general, the bases of these clouds are about 3,000 to 4,000 feet above the ground.

In fair or good weather, cumulus clouds tend to remain small, so that their vertical height is generally less than 1 mile. Why is their growth arrested? As each cloud extends upward, it encounters dry air that mixes with the cloud and causes the cloud droplets to evaporate. At times, however, very warm moist air swirls upward through the cloud column and a series of complex changes takes place, causing the rising air to be accelerated upward more rapidly. Then the cloud grows to great heights, often extending into the stratosphere. Such clouds, called cumulonimbus, ordinarily produce lightning, thunder, heavy rains, and hail. A more detailed discussion of these clouds appears in Chapter IV.

Stratiform clouds are formed by upward air movements that are largely horizontal. Often, large masses of these clouds are formed when maritime tropical air masses are lifted slowly as they pass over other air masses.

A typical stratiform cloud is stratus, which is a uniform sheetlike mass that appears as a fog lifted off the ground. The predominant features of stratus clouds are their relative thinness and layered, or flat, appearance. If you can recall mornings that have been dull and gray, and sometimes drizzly, you know what stratus clouds are like, for such mornings are typical of stratus clouds. On such mornings, the sun usually "burns" through well before noon; then the clouds dissipate and a sunny day follows.

Cirrus clouds are thin, featherlike clouds that are always

found at great heights—usually above 20,000 feet. These clouds, which usually appear crystal white, are always composed of ice crystals. Similar to these clouds are the trails formed by high-flying jets. These white trails, called contrails (condensation trails), are composed of ice crystals produced when water vapor resulting from combustion in the engines freezes when it hits the extremely cold air at high altitudes.

At sunrise and sunset cirrus clouds reflect red and yellow hues that contribute to brilliantly colored sunrises and sunsets. When cirrus clouds are scattered across the sky, they indicate fair weather. If they are seen advancing across the sky as a thin widespread sheet that thickens during the day, they are harbingers of stormy weather.

Oftentimes, clouds have characteristics of each main type. Then these clouds are given names that indicate their overall appearance. For example, a layer of clouds with cumuliform characteristics would be called stratocumulus. An ice cloud composed of globular masses would be labeled cirrocumulus. And a stratiform "ice cloud" would be called cirrostratus.

Weather scientists also apply names to clouds that identify them according to height. Thus, a layered cloud at middle altitudes—about 6,500 to 20,000 feet—would be called altostratus, alto meaning middle. And a puffy cloud in the middle range is classified as altocumulus.

A special category has been considered for cumulonimbus clouds, which you recall have great vertical development. Since these clouds generally extend from a few thousand feet or less at the base, and up to the cirrus range, they could be classed as clouds with great vertical development. However, since cumulonimbus clouds originate at low levels they are considered low clouds. The uniqueness of these clouds is that the cloud particles in the upper portions are composed of ice crystals, whereas the lower portions are composed of liquid droplets. The anvil top of a cumulonimbus cloud is believed by some to be caused by the precipitation of moisture triggered by the condensation of supercooled moisture on ice nuclei. This disrupts the upward billowing of the cauliflower-shaped cloud. The flattened top may also be explained by the fact that these clouds penetrate into the stratosphere, where the stable air deters upward growth. Ordinarily the anvil top points in the general direction of movement of the main cloud mass.

Two unusual clouds are nacreous and noctilucent clouds. These clouds, observed primarily in the polar and subpolar regions, occur at extreme heights. Nacreous – "mother-of-pearl" – clouds are usually situated at heights of 70,000 to 100,000 feet. These clouds are believed to be composed of small particles of water or ice. Noctilucent – "night-glowing" – clouds are usually found at altitudes of 250,000 to 300,000 feet. These clouds, which occasionally may be seen as glimmering silvery-blue bands in the early morning or early evening sky, are believed to be made of meteoric dust.

II

Rain

After water has been evaporated from the earth's surface
and forms clouds, it may return to the earth as rain, snow,
hail, or other forms of precipitation. This is a continuous
process. It involves the evaporation of large quantities of
water that move into the air. This moisture-laden air eventually gives up its moisture as precipitation. The water, returning to the earth as rain (or snow), ordinarily soaks into the
land and eventually flows to the sea and evaporates once
more, to repeat the cycle. This cycle is named the water, or
hydrologic cycle.

Man depends on the continuation of the water cycle for
replenishment of water he uses for agriculture, industry,
commerce, and household needs. If this process should
cease or be disrupted, it would be difficult for man to continue
his existence on earth. For example, the lack of rainfall
would result in diminishing food supplies within a short
time. A famous example of such an effect on a relatively
small scale is the noted "dust bowl" region of the Great
Plains (Fig. 1). During the early 1930's a series of droughts
struck this region. Crops withered and died. Millions of
acres of farmland lay bare with the dry, loose topsoil exposed
to the wind Moderate to strong winds lifted the unprotected

topsoil and carried it away. At times, airborne soil particles, as fine as dust, darkened the sky. The wind-transported particles were observed as far away as the Atlantic seaboard.

FIG. 1 *Duststorms in abandoned farm in 1930's.*

Although the disastrous dust storms of the 1930's were attributed to drought conditions, the real cause lay in poor farming practices. Before World War I, the dust-bowl region was covered with grasses that needed little moisture to survive. During the war, however, American farmers found it profitable to plow under the grasses of the Great Plains and plant wheat. Fortunately, rainfall during this time was more than adequate for wheat crops, and the farmlands yielded rich harvests. But several years later a series of droughts caused the crops to die, and the region lay unprotected. The crop failures resulted in a triple disaster—millions of tons of topsoil were stripped from the land, numerous farmers became impoverished, and a vast army of refugees drifted to other places seeking employment, often at near-starvation wages. This migration is well documented by John Steinbeck's depiction of the Okies in his famous novel *The Grapes of Wrath.*

Even when man does not disrupt nature, he still has many problems associated with the lack of, or even excesses of, precipitation. Fortunately, many places on the earth receive rainfall adequate to their needs. Shortages and excesses are relatively uncommon and those regions thrive.

Clouds and Precipitation

In Chapter I we discussed the various factors involved in cloud formation—how precipitation depends upon the formation of clouds in the atmosphere. For example, regions such as the doldrums, where cloudy days are common, tend to have higher average precipitation records for the year than places where cloudy days are uncommon. An example of such cloudy places are Belém and Manaos in the Amazon Valley. During a typical year Belém receives about 94 inches of rain and Manaos receives about 65 inches. By comparison, if we look at the rainfall records of relatively cloudless regions, we find the average rainfall is extremely low. For example, Yuma, Arizona, which is largely cloudless during the year, has an average annual rainfall of about 3 inches. And, over much of the Sahara, the average yearly rainfall is less than 5 inches. This condition holds true for other desert regions such as the Sonora Desert of the United States and Mexico, the Atacama-Peruvian desert in South America, and the Australian desert.

The general relationships between cloudy days and precipitation can be seen in Fig. 2, which shows the average annual precipitation throughout the contiguous United States. Differences in cloudiness and rainfall depend on a number of factors, including winds and pressure, accessibility of moisture, and the configuration of the land. The effect these and other factors have on precipitation over a region can be demonstrated by the following examples of extremes in rainfall:

Place	Average Annual Rainfall (inches)
Mount Waialeale, Hawaii	472
Cherrapunji, India	426
Cameroon Peak, Nigeria	400
Belém, Brazil	243
Calama, Chile	no rainfall ever recorded
Iquique, Chile	0.12 (approx.)
Aswan, Egypt	almost none

The above figures can be misleading since they represent the average rainfall over many years. For example, at Iquique, Chile, the average rainfall is stated as 0.12 inch each year. Actually, over a period of five years rain fell only once in a brief shower that dropped 0.6 inch of rain. Thus, dividing 0.6 by 5 gives an "expected" annual rainfall of 0.12 inch. And in Thar, India, where the average rainfall is about 5 inches, as much as 34 inches have fallen over a

Average Annual Precipitation

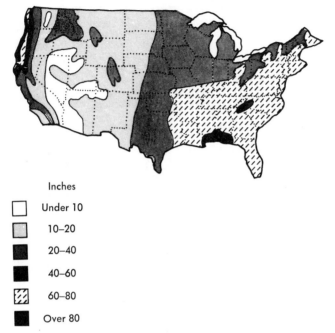

Inches

☐ Under 10

▨ 10–20

■ 20–40

■ 40–60

▨ 60–80

■ Over 80

FIG. 2

two-day period. Rainfall over desert regions has another peculiarity: often rain falling from clouds evaporates completely before reaching the ground.

Although weather scientists have a number of explanations for the differences in cloudiness and precipitation, they cannot predict exactly when and how clouds may form and release their moisture in the form of rain or snow. Their attempts to predict where and when precipitation will occur, and in what amounts, are hindered by changes in the atmosphere that go undetected because of the limited number of weather observatories scattered around the world.

The largest number of official weather observatories are found in the industrial nations of the world—over 600 in the United States alone. Yet this is a relatively small number compared to the huge expanse of the United States. In underdeveloped regions, the number of stations is so few that huge portions of the atmosphere go unmeasured. Relatively few stations cover regions such as Siberia, Antarctica, and the Amazon. A relative handful of permanent weather stations and a scattering of ships make regular observations of the atmosphere above the ocean, although the ocean not only covers over 70 percent of the earth's surface but is also the major source of the moisture that produces clouds and precipitation over land areas.

Scientists are also thwarted by the immensity of the atmosphere and the limited number of probes they can make of its vast depths. The data gathered by probes such as instrumented balloons, aircraft, rockets, and satellites are extremely valuable, yet sparse, when we consider the numerous portions of the atmosphere that go unobserved by scientific instruments.

Although scientists have been somewhat limited in their studies of the atmosphere, they have learned much about the nature of precipitation that may occur in isolated instances, or as part of weather systems that move across the land. Meteorologists have particularly concerned themselves with the physical mechanisms at work in the atmosphere that result in the formation of clouds and precipitation. They have made intensive studies of the structure of clouds and the particles that compose them (see Chapter I). And they have tried to understand under what conditions clouds release their water vapor as precipitation.

Rain and Cloud Droplets

Over 2,000 years ago, a noted Roman, Lucretius, believed that rain was caused by the wind pressing against clouds swollen with moisture. Although Lucretius' thoughts were erroneous, it has only been in recent years that anyone has come close to explaining what causes rain. And this is easy to understand, because the formation of raindrops from cloud droplets is extremely difficult to observe. To understand this problem, visualize a million cloud droplets combining to form one raindrop inside a cloud. Since a typical cloud droplet may be about 10 microns (0.0004 in.) in diameter, you can appreciate the complexity of this problem.

Much of the research that has been undertaken to understand the nature of rain has been done in the twentieth century. Questions scientists have asked are: How does rain form? How big are raindrops? What shape do raindrops have? The first question is the most important and the most difficult to answer. Although scientists believe they have reasonably satisfactory answers to this question, there is still no complete explanation for the occurrence of rain.

The problem of measuring raindrops presented a less formidable obstacle to understanding the nature of rain. Since raindrops are "manufactured products" that represent the end result of processes at work in clouds, they may hold the secret of the formation of raindrops in their size, shape, composition, or other characteristics. Accordingly, much research has been done on the characteristics of raindrops.

One of the simplest and most interesting raindrop research projects was undertaken at the turn of the century by William Bentley, a Vermont farmer. Although Bentley's method of studying raindrops was simple, it was ingenious and his results were remarkable. His method involved placing pans of flour outdoors briefly during rainstorms. Falling raindrops were "soaked up" by the flour and produced small "balls" of dough. Then Bentley measured their diameters. The next step was to find out what size drops would produce the dough balls. Since Bentley could not measure the size of falling raindrops, he set up apparatus that would produce various-sized drops of water. Then, from various heights, he released drops of water into pans of flour and measured the size of the dough balls produced. By comparing the results obtained by measuring natural raindrops and artificial raindrops, Bentley concluded that raindrops come in different sizes. In addition, by studying the dough balls he reasoned that melted snow may be one possible source of raindrops. This deduction was remarkable, as you will see later in this chapter.

As a result of the work of a number of researchers using the flour-pan technique and other methods of measuring raindrops — such as various types of coated screens and absorbent paper upon which raindrops left their impressions, and electronic scanners — scientists have established the range of raindrop sizes. At the lower level, drops are 0.008 inch (0.2 mm) in diameter; at the upper level drops are about 0.25 inch (6 mm) in diameter.

Shapes of Raindrops

In addition to studying size, researchers have delved into the shape of raindrops. Of course, an artist may depict raindrops as tear-shaped objects, but this is far from reality. Actual photographs of falling raindrops show them to take on a variety of shapes — none of them tear-shaped.

The shape of a raindrop depends upon its size. The smaller the drop, the more spherical it becomes. Very large drops are generally flattened on the bottom and dome-shaped on top. The shape of the drop is controlled by various forces, such as surface tension and air pressing against the falling drop. The effect of surface tension is to cause the drop to assume the smallest size possible. This happens because the surface molecules of a raindrop are attracted by the molecules below and at the sides. As a result, the center of the drop becomes the focus for the pulling forces and the drop assumes a spherical shape. This effect can be seen by placing drops of water from a medicine dropper on talcum powder. The water forms spherical droplets since the inward-pulling forces within the water drop are greater than the attractive force of the talcum powder. A similar effect is seen when raindrops bead up on a freshly waxed automobile. Can you explain this?

As raindrops fall, the air presses against them and tends to flatten them at the bottom. Air rushing past the curved sides of the drop tends to reduce the air pressure on these surfaces so that the drop tends to bulge outward. The degree to which a raindrop is distorted depends on the size of the raindrop. In very small drops, the surface molecules are strongly attracted to the center of the drop by the attractive forces within. This strong attraction for the surface molecules is much larger than the forces that tend to distort the drops; therefore, small drops tend to remain nearly spherical in shape (Fig. 3a). As raindrops increase in size, the inward attractive forces acting upon the surface molecules are less effective in holding them in place. In addition, larger drops fall faster than smaller drops, so that there is an increase in the outside forces acting upon them. Thus, as drops increase in size the inward-pulling forces become less effective and the outward forces become more effective. The result — large drops, generally 3 mm to about 5 mm in diameter, flatten out on the bottom and bulge strongly on the sides (Fig. 3b). Drops 5 mm and up tend to distort in the same

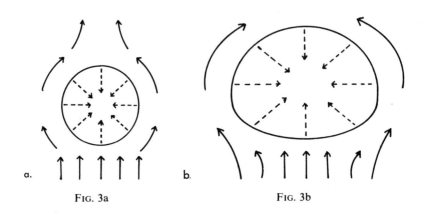

FIG. 3a   FIG. 3b

way — but the outside forces overcome the inside forces and the drops are torn apart.

If we could look within clouds we would find a large range in the size and number of cloud droplets. Ordinarily, cumuliform clouds have larger cloud droplets than stratiform clouds. In the typical small cumulus cloud seen overhead, cloud droplets are usually less than 50 microns (0.002 in.) in diameter. In large cumulus clouds, droplets are usually over 50 microns in diameter. By comparison, in stratiform clouds, the typical cloud droplets are several times smaller than those in cumuliform clouds.

Theories of Rain

The fact that one to eight million cloud particles are in one raindrop can be verified by measurements. And the fact that cloud droplets form raindrops can also be verified by analyzing clouds. But how cloud droplets combine to form raindrops has yet to be explained fully by scientists. To explain raindrop formation, a number of theories have been proposed. Currently, two theories in common acceptance are the coalescence theory and the ice-crystal theory.

Coalescence and Raindrop Formation

Coalescence involves a fairly simple process in which cloud droplets combine to form larger droplets as a result of collisions (Fig. 4). Ordinarily, cloud droplets are so small that they fall through the air very slowly and their chances of colliding are small. However, cloud droplets vary in size so that some fall faster than others. Large droplets—about 100 microns in diameter—fall about 25 times faster than small droplets—about 20 microns in diameter. Thus, the larger droplets, falling much faster than the rest—about 26 cm/sec versus 1 cm/sec—overtake them and collide with them. As the droplets coalesce, not only do they increase in size, but their ability to collect more droplets also increases. If the falling droplet is inside a rather thick cloud, such as a cumulus cloud, it may gather enough droplets to produce a raindrop that falls to earth. The typical raindrop falls about 3 meters per sec, or about 7 miles per hour.

The coalescence process may depend in part upon the presence of salt nuclei carried into the clouds from the sea. These nuclei, you recall from Chapter I, have a strong affinity for water vapor. Thus, within a cloud they would

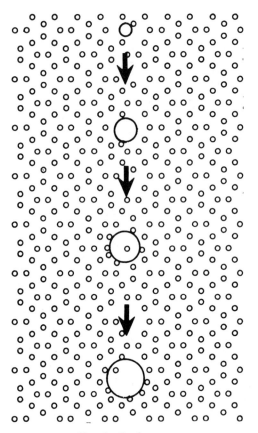

FIG. 4 *Coalescence*

grow larger than ordinary cloud droplets. Evidence supporting this theory comes from observations of clouds over tropical regions, where strongly hygroscopic nuclei are present in the air. This condition would be especially true in the air over tropical oceans, where sea-salt particles are abundant.

The Ice-Crystal Theory

Prior to World War II the ice-crystal theory was accepted as the best explanation for precipitation. Essentially, this theory assumes that ice crystals must be present in clouds for rain to fall. During the war, however, numerous airplanes flew above rain clouds over tropical regions and they made a significant observation — often air temperatures in the clouds were well above freezing. At these temperatures ice crystals could not form. Accordingly, the coalescence theory, in which liquid droplets combine to form raindrops, was proposed as another theory to explain the formation of rain. But, strange as it may seem, what appears to be the simpler process — collisions — was proposed many years after the more complicated ice-crystal theory was proposed. Can you imagine why the ice-crystal process is more complicated? Here is a hint — it has to do with the differences in "pressure" at the surface of water droplets and ice crystals.

The ice-crystal process depends on the presence of supercooled water droplets and ice crystals in a cloud. This condition is likely to develop in the upper levels of thick clouds over the middle latitude. Consider water droplets being uplifted inside a cumuliform cloud. In the lower portion of the cloud, where temperatures are in the neighborhood of 10° F. (−10° C.), the droplets would be in the liquid state. As they are lifted to higher altitudes where temperatures are lower, some of the supercooled droplets freeze and form ice crystals. These ice crystals become nuclei that attract molecules of water vapor from the water droplets. This exchange upsets the balance within the cloud; now cloud droplets give up moisture, and the ice crystals grow larger. The enlarged ice crystals fall and collide with other ice crystals and the smaller supercooled droplets; upon contact with ice crystals, the supercooled droplets freeze. In your own experience you may have seen a somewhat similar effect in the wintertime when cold rain freezes upon contact with car windshields. If you can visualize this process, you can see how it is similar to the coalescent process described earlier. As this process continues, then, the ice crystals become too large to be supported by the upcurrents within the cloud. Thus, the collection of ice crystals falls from the cloud and drifts downward as snow. If temperatures from the cloud downward remain near or below freezing, a snowfall is experienced on the ground. At times, however, a temperature inversion may exist in the atmosphere. Then snowflakes may fall into regions of progressively higher temperatures as they float downward, and they melt. They may reach the ground as very wet snow or rain depending upon air temperatures and the thickness of the warm layer of the atmosphere.

Rainfall and Pollutants

In recent years, scientists have noted differences in weather brought about by sprawling urban centers where industrial plants, large buildings, parking lots, paved streets, highways, and automobiles contribute in various ways to disrupting the normal weather patterns of these regions. Among their observations is the fact that metropolitan areas get more rain, clouds, and fog than suburban areas. Yet the suburban areas do not go unscathed, for the "spill over" from the urban areas extends outward many miles. A noted example of such a region is La Porte, Indiana, which is situated about 30 miles from the large steel mills of Gary, Indiana, and South Chicago. From 1951 through 1965 the steel business boomed and so did the steel-plant furnaces at Gary and South Chicago. During this period La Porte experienced great increases in thunderstorms, hailstorms, and general precipitation. According to weather records, thunderstorms increased by 38 percent, hailstorms by 246 percent, and other precipitation by 31 percent. Scientists believe that pollutants from the steel-producing centers, carried over La Porte by the wind, triggered the local atmosphere to release its moisture. The explanation—the pollutants added to the air hygroscopic particles that stimulate the formation of clouds. In a somewhat similar situation, a community in the Pacific Northwest experienced increased rainfall after a large sawmill began operations upwind from it.

Interestingly, scientists have found that the highest incidence of cloudiness and rainfall in urban areas occurs during the workweek. This difference can be explained by the fact that industrial plants are ordinarily closed down, or on reduced shifts, during weekends. Thus, over the weekend, two sources of air pollutants—industrial chimneys and automobile exhausts—are greatly reduced. Furthermore, during the workweek large amounts of heat are produced by industrial furnaces, air conditioners, motor vehicles, and other sources. This heat causes an increase in air temperatures, which are already higher than ordinary because the "concreted" and "asphalted" urban areas are good absorbers of the sun's heat. Weather scientists believe that the addition of man-made heat to weather systems has an adverse effect on weather fronts in such areas.

III

Snow

Of all the forms of precipitation, snow is usually the most beautiful sight to behold – if you are a child! For adults, this may be true when snowfalls are relatively light. When heavy snowfalls occur, however, they present a serious threat to life and property. In addition, the loss to the economy in disrupted traffic and snow removal is substantial. For example, in December, 1947, a snowstorm dropped about 2 feet of snow on New York City. The cost of snow removal was $4,500,000; fortunately, the loss of life was low.

Just two years after New York City was brought to a standstill by that record snowfall, the West was struck by snowstorms and blizzards that raged on and off for nearly two months. Farms, towns, even cities were virtually paralyzed as snowfall followed snowfall. Numerous motorists were trapped in automobiles; many died before they could be rescued. More than fifty trains were snowbound between Nebraska and Idaho. With the lives of hundreds of thousands of people and millions of sheep and cattle threatened by the raging storms, an emergency was declared. In came the National Guard and regular army units with all types of equipment that could be used for snow removal – even tanks. They opened highways, rescued stranded motorists, and delivered emergency fuel and food and other supplies. The toll taken by this storm was 200 human lives and an estimated million sheep and cattle.

For New York City, the heavy snowfall of 1947 was unusual; the average yearly snowfall in the city is about 30 inches. By comparison, in more northern regions of the East, such as sections of Vermont and New Hampshire, the average yearly snowfall is three to four times that of New York City.

Snow Regions

The regions of greatest snow accumulation ordinarily lie in the paths followed by winter storms as they travel eastward across the United States (Fig. 1). The large accumulations experienced in the Northeast section of the United States can be attributed largely to two factors: (1) most eastward moving storms curve northward as they approach the eastern half of the country, and (2) below-freezing temperatures are common in this region.

In addition, large amounts of moisture from the Great Lakes region and especially from the Gulf of Mexico are available for the formation of snow. In the Great Lakes region, the snowfalls are often precipitated by continental polar (cP) air, or arctic (A) air, moving downward from Canada and across the relatively warm, moist surface of the lakes.

The Gulf of Mexico, being far larger and warmer than the Great Lakes, supplies far greater quantities of moisture to the atmosphere. As the warm, moist tropical air (mT) from the Gulf moves north and eastward, it meets cold dry (cP) air moving south and eastward from Canada. Often these air masses meet in the colder latitudes where New York and the

New England states are situated. Along the opposing fronts of these air masses, moist air is lifted upward by denser air masses. The water vapor in the uplifted mass crystallizes and returns to earth as snow.

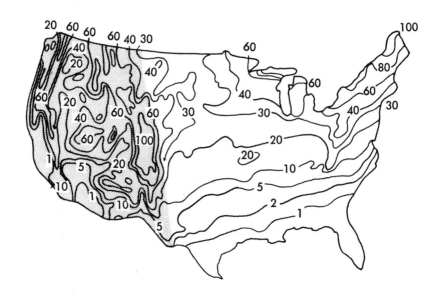

Average Annual Snow Distribution

Fig. 1

Much heavier snowfalls are common in the mountain systems of the western portion of the United States. For example, in sections of Washington, California, Oregon, and Colorado the average yearly snowfalls are 200 inches. In some mountainous regions, snow accumulations are staggering. For example, in the vicinity of Yosemite Park, 450 inches (about 38 feet) of snow have fallen in one winter. And at Summit, California, about 100 years ago, nearly 800 inches (about 66 feet) of snow fell in one winter.

Heavy snowfalls often occur in mountainous regions for two reasons: first, mountainous regions are usually colder than regions near sea level; and second, mountains act as wedges that force air masses to rise as they move against their

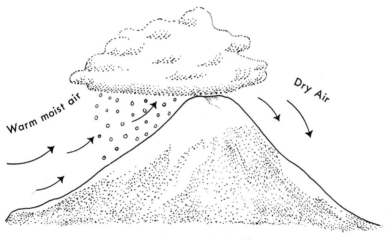

Orographic Uplift.

Fig. 2

steep surfaces. The forcing upward of masses of air by raised ground surfaces is called orographic uplift. Orographic uplift is especially effective in producing heavy snowfalls in the high mountain ranges of the West (Fig. 2).

In the winter, warm, moist Pacific air drifts eastward toward the Rockies and other Western mountain ranges. When the moisture-laden air reaches these mountain ranges, it undergoes orographic uplift and climbs steadily to high elevations, where condensation occurs. Shortly thereafter, the thickening clouds release their moisture as snow. Thus, heavy snows fall on the windward or western portions of the mountain systems. Strong winds often carry part of the newly fallen snow to lower regions on the leeward sides of the mountains. Accumulations in valleys, leeward of mountains, are often of great depths. A region noted for incredible snowfalls is the coastal mountain ranges extending from Alaska to the state of Washington. Along portions of these mountains moist, warm air from the Pacific Ocean is brought onshore by prevailing winds over the ocean. In the path of the moisture-laden air are two barriers: the high coastal mountains that present a permanent barrier blocking the path of the onshore winds; and the polar front, which is a relatively permanent barrier in the path of the onshore winds. The combination of these two uplifting agents—the mass of high mountains and the mass of cold air—results in great snowfalls. For example, at Thompson Pass in the coastal mountains of southern Alaska snowfalls averaged 600 inches (50 feet) a year for a decade. In the winter of 1952–53 nearly 1,000 inches of snow were recorded.

Farther south, in the state of Washington, lofty Mount Rainier, the highest mountain in the state, may hold the world's record for the deepest accumulation of snow in one winter. In 1955–56, at Paradise Valley along the south slope of Mt. Rainier, the Paradise Ranger Station recorded 1,000 inches (83 feet, 4 inches) of snowfall.

Although the records set at Thompson Pass and Paradise Valley through one winter are incredible, other mountain locations have also had prodigious snowfalls, but over shorter periods. For example, in 1911, at the Tamarack reservoir, near Lake Tahoe in the Sierra Nevada, a 390-inch (about 33 foot) snowfall was recorded for a single month—the month of

January. And in January of 1952 a raging snowstorm dropped about 9 feet of snow in this region over a four-day period. Ordinarily, the snowfalls in this region are in the neighborhood of 60 feet for an entire winter. The record snowfall of 1952 imperiled a passenger train, the Southern Pacific's noted streamliner the City of San Francisco, which was traveling westward at the time. During the storm, the train became snowbound when the powerful diesel engines could no longer pull the cars through the ever-deepening snow. Aboard the stranded train were 226 passengers. The storm had not only closed the railroad to all traffic but also blocked all highway traffic. Thus, as the storm raged about them, the passengers anxiously awaited rescue teams. On the fourth day of their entrapment, powerful rotary snowplows cut through the massive wall of snow, and the frightening experience ended for the passengers and crew.

Long before railroads cut their way through these mountainous regions, settlers followed the natural valleys that made possible the traversing of the rugged mountain terrain. In early November of 1846, a wagon train of 79 settlers, under the leadership of George Donner, was trapped by a snowstorm several miles east of the site (just north of Lake Tahoe) where the San Francisco streamliner became snowbound. As wagons and tow animals bogged down, the entire wagon train became engulfed by the raging storm. More storms followed, blizzards howled, and snow piled up in drifts 30 to 40 feet high. The wagon train was trapped for the winter. Crude shelters were built to withstand the bitter cold, and food was carefully rationed. As weeks dragged into months, the food supplies—even the tow animals—had been consumed. In grim desperation, to keep themselves alive, the settlers ate the flesh of their own dead. With the sense of impending doom upon them, several volunteers made their way across the trackless snow for help from the settlements below. About half of them got through, and rescue parties were sent out. After several attempts, a rescue party finally reached the snowbound pioneers. Of the original 79 settlers, 45 survived the terrible ordeal. A noted memento of the tragedy that befell the settlers is Donner Pass, which is named after George Donner, the leader of the hapless wagon train.

Snowfalls and Glaciers

Snowfalls are not limited to northerly or near-northerly regions. In Africa, Mt. Kenya and Mt. Kilimanjaro (volcanic mountains) have snow-covered peaks the year round. And Mt. Kenya lies just about on the equator, whereas Kilimanjaro is about 200 miles south of the equator. However, both mountains are over 3 miles high; Kenya is about 17,000 feet high, Kilimanjaro about 19,000 feet.

Mt. Kenya is especially notable, for though it is at the equator, a large glacier has formed on its peak as a result of regular snowfalls. The moisture that feeds the Kenya glacier originates in the steaming jungles below.

In North America, glaciers are situated principally on the mountain ranges of the West Coast area extending from Alaska to the state of Washington. There are hundreds, possibly thousands, of glaciers scattered throughout this great range of mountains. The numerous glaciers of this mountainous region demonstrate vividly the effect of high elevations that cause moisture-laden air to give up its water vapor in the form of snow.

Some of the largest and longest mountain glaciers of the world are found in the mountain ranges bordering the Gulf of Alaska. Noted glaciers in this region are the Hubbard Glacier, the Logan Glacier, and the Malaspina Glacier (a piedmont glacier). The longest of these—about 75 miles long—is the Hubbard Glacier. Farther south, the principal glacier areas are situated in the general region occupied by Jasper, Banff, and Yoho National Parks of Canada. These parks are situated

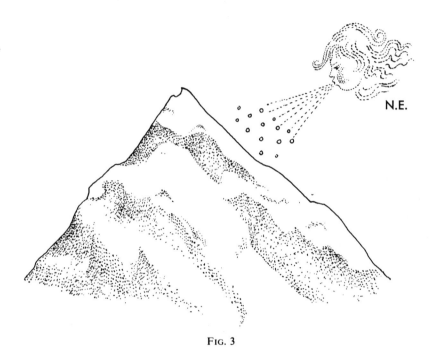

FIG. 3

approximately 150 to 300 miles north of Washington, Idaho, and Montana.

In the United States, hundreds of small glaciers occupy bowl-shaped erosion features called cirques. They are situated primarily on the north and east sides of mountains. Snow swept off the mountaintops by strong winds is the major source of snow for these glaciers (Fig. 3) which are principally situated in Glacier National Park, Montana, and the Wind River Range in Wyoming.

Have you ever heard it said: "If it gets too cold, it cannot snow." Although fewer people make this statement nowadays, it was once a popular misconception. The fact that it snows at the South Pole and other extremely cold places belies the statement. Records indicate that snow has fallen at temperatures below −50° F. (−46° C.). However, at very low temperatures the air can hold very little moisture. Accordingly, snowfalls in extremely cold places are relatively light and individual snowflakes are small in size. When we consider the size and thickness of the ice sheet covering Antarctica — 5,100,000 square miles and about 10,000 feet thick — we may wonder how so much ice could accumulate. The answer is quite simple — most of the snow that falls never melts because temperatures in Antarctica are well below zero. If the snow, which has become mostly ice as a result of compression, were melted, the oceans would probably rise more than 200 feet.

Water Supplies and Snow

Although the water in Antarctica is locked within crystals of ice, it represents a possible future source of fresh water, as it contains about 64 percent of the world's freshwater supplies. It has been suggested already that large broken-off sections of the Antarctic be towed to places in serious need of fresh water.

Water from glaciers makes up an important part of the world's freshwater supplies. Melt waters from glaciers all over the world are used for irrigation, hydroelectricity, municipal supplies — drinking, cooking, sanitation — and numerous other uses. In the United States and Canada many municipalities and farms depend upon streams pouring out of glaciers for their water supplies. Especially interesting is the fact that Tacoma, Washington, depends upon the surging waters from the Nisqually Glacier on Mt. Rainier for the production of its electricity.

The melt waters of glaciers coursing downward from the mountains eventually return to the sea, from which they had been transported many years earlier in the form of water vapor. In time, some of this water vapor returns to the glaciers as snow, where once more each snow crystal will be compressed into the solid mass of glacier ice.

In many localities winter snowfalls provide a major part of the water supplies needed for all uses. In the West, especially, almost all of the water supplies come from snow that has fallen in the mountains during the winter. In the spring, the deep snows slowly melt and produce numerous streams that pour down the mountains. Much of this water is diverted into reservoirs and irrigation canals, to be released when needed. Throughout the West, crops such as peaches, oranges, lemons, cotton, dates, lettuce, tomatoes, and other farm produce would not grow if it were not for the melt waters of winter snows. The highly productive Central Valley of California would be a vast desert if melt waters from winter snows were not available. And numerous other localities in the West could not exist if it were not for the melt waters supplying rivers such as the Colorado and the Columbia, and for the melt waters stored in the vast reservoirs behind dams such as Hoover Dam in Nevada. The importance of snow-fed rivers for water supplies is demonstrated by the fact that the Colorado delivers trillions of gallons of water annually. The Columbia and its tributary, the Snake River, provide ten times more water than the Colorado.

Since melt water is so important to the West, the government employs more than one thousand snow surveyors who traverse the snow fields and measure the snow for its water content. One of their methods is rather simple. A hollow tube is pushed through the snow to the ground beneath. When the tube is removed it is weighed on a special scale, which indicates the water content of the snow. The collected data are recorded and then transmitted to a central office. From the thousands of reports received, scientists calculate the amount of melt water that will be available for use when the spring thaws release the water locked in the crystals of snow.

When we consider the vast amount of water that is derived from snowfalls we should keep in mind that an average snowfall of one foot contains about one inch of precipitation. Thus, when 100 inches of snow accumulate we can anticipate a runoff of 10 inches of rain. Fortunately, melting is relatively slow; if all the snow melted in, say, one day, the resulting floods would be disastrous. As it is, water released by relatively slow melting often creates flooding problems in the springtime.

An important factor in the slow melting of snow is the albedo, or reflecting property of snow. Fresh clean snow reflects about 87 percent of the incoming sunlight. This ability to reflect light so well is determined by the crystals of ice that make up each snowflake. When viewed beneath the microscope, individual snow crystals usually appear to have lacy patterns with a fundamental hexagonal form, as shown in Fig. 4. A closer look reveals minute crystal prisms, which are arranged in an infinite variety of patterns. Sunlight reflected from each of these prisms forms a rainbow of colors that are too fine to be distinguished by the human eye. At times, however, one can catch a glimpse of a pinpoint of sparkling colors in clean snow and bright sunlight. Except for such rare glimpses of color, the total effect of fresh snow seen in sunlight is a brilliant whiteness.

Fig. 4 *Snow Crystals*

Snow-Crystal Shapes

Probably one of the most common statements made about snow is: "No two snowflakes are alike." This is difficult to comprehend when we take into consideration the number of snowflakes that fall in one snowstorm—countless trillions!

Even though we can never get to study each individual snow-flake that falls, we know that individual crystals are commonly six-sided polygons (hexagons), and it is believed that the difference in design based on the hexagon is infinite. Yet, of the myriad snow crystals that form, they are limited to the distinct shapes graphically represented in Fig. 4. Drawings of actual snowflakes with these distinct shapes are shown in the graphic representation. Not included in the grouping are other types of crystals, such as irregular crystals, which have less distinct shapes; snow pellets, which appear as tiny snowballs; and sleet and hail, which form differently than snow crystals. Most of us are familiar with sleet and hail that may fall to the earth at different times of the year. Sleet, as you may know, is commonly a winter phenomenon; hail is usually a spring and summer phenomenon. Snow pellets, also called graupel, are a form of snow that most people mistake for hail; in fact, snow pellets are often referred to as soft hail. The formation of snow pellets depends upon the sweeping up of numerous cloud droplets by a stellar crystal as it falls through a cloud. Upon contact with the arms of the snow crystal, the droplets freeze and the result is a snow crystal encased in ice, which appears as a minute snowball.

Snow Crystals Reveal the Nature of Clouds

Snow crystals are silent messengers from the clouds, because the size and shape of each crystal indicate the temperature and humidity conditions within a cloud. In the laboratory, scientists can duplicate every type of snow crystal by controlling the temperature and humidity inside a special device called a cold chamber. Of the two factors, temperature appears to have the greatest influence on the shape of snow crystals. This is demonstrated by the following list showing the type of snow crystal that forms within distinct temperature ranges:

Snow-Crystal Shape	Temperature Range
plate	0° C. to −3° C. (32° F. to 26.6° F.)
needle	−3° C. to −5° C. (26.6° F. to 23° F.)
hollow plate	−5° C. to −8° C. (23° F. to 17.6° F.)
plate	−8° C. to −12° C. (17.6° F. to 10.4° F.)
dendrite (stellar)	−12° C. to −16° C. (10.4° C. to 3.2° F.)
plate	−16° C. to −25° C. (3.2° F. to −13° F.)
columns	−25° C. to −50° C. (−13° F. to −58° F.)

These temperature ranges are quite critical. For example, a needle-shaped crystal growing at −3° C. will stop growing as a needle and form a plate at its end if the temperature rises to −2° C. As can be readily seen, then, the shape of a snow crystal provides a record of the temperature conditions it encountered within a cloud.

As we have seen, temperature changes are most influential in determining the form of snow crystals. Typically the size of individual crystals ranges from about 0.008 inch to about 0.5 inch in diameter. The approximate ranges in size for some crystals are as follows:

Snow Crystals	Size in Inches* (approx.)
plates	0.01 to 0.13
needles	0.25 to 0.37 (length)
dendrites (stellars)	0.03 to 0.50
columns (hexagonal and capped)	0.02 to 0.13

* For comparison purposes ◯ 0.13 in. diam. ◯ 0.25 in. diam.

0.50 in. diam.

As snow crystals fall through clouds, they often collide and stick together. In this way, different sized snowflakes are produced. When clouds are thick, the supply of water molecules is high, temperatures are near freezing (about 32° F.), there is rapid growth, and crystals with dendritic or fernlike arms are likely to form. These crystals have a tendency to clump together and form very large, moist snowflakes, which may contain fifty or more interlocked crystals. At times snowflakes the size of your palm are formed. The record snowflake is said to have measured about 8 inches across! By contrast, in extremely cold places such as the polar regions and at high altitudes where subzero temperatures are common and the moisture content of the air is very low, snowfalls tend to be composed of very small, dense, and compact-shaped crystals. An interesting sight that can be seen on cold winter mornings when a blanket of fog covers the earth are very small crystals sparkling in the cold air. If you have ever observed this, you understand why meteorologists describe it as "diamond dust."

As one would expect, in a cloud layer 2 miles thick, with relatively large temperature differences within its mass, a variety of snow crystals and snowflakes are produced. The snowfall that reaches the ground contains the wide variety of crystal forms produced at different temperatures — plates, stellars, needles, columns — and probably combination forms.

Although the actual process that results in the formation of snow crystals is reasonably well understood, weather scientists are still doing research to understand better the mechanism that triggers clouds to produce snow. One thing scientists know is that snow forms in clouds where water droplets composing the cloud are at 32° F. or lower. In fact, according to observations cloud droplets can remain in the liquid form at temperatures near −39° F. The clouds from

which we get the greatest snowfalls have temperatures ranging from about 14° F. to 32° F.

Snow-Crystal Formation

Some scientists speculate that snow crystals are produced
by a physical reaction involving supercooled particles (nuclei)
in clouds and water droplets. They believe that the supercooled water particles freeze when they come in contact with
the extremely cold nuclei. In the laboratory, scientists have
duplicated this process by adding a piece of dry ice (frozen
carbon dioxide) to a chamber containing a supercooled cloud.
The addition of the dry ice, which has a temperature of
−146° F., triggered the cloud to produce ice crystals. In
other experiments, scientists found that the addition of
other extremely cold foreign substances, such as metal rods
and rabbit hairs, to a supercooled cloud could produce similar
results. These discoveries led researchers to wonder whether
they could produce similar results with natural clouds. In
1946, Vincent Schaefer, one of the pioneers in ice-crystal
research, dropped pellets of dry ice into a mass of supercooled altostratus located nearly 3 miles up. Just before releasing the pellets, Schaefer found no evidence of ice crystals. Temperatures within the cloud were about 0° F. As the
pellets were distributed through the cloud it began to churn;
within minutes snow fell from the entire cloud. The snow
evaporated before it reached the ground.

In nature, the types of particles that are likely to act as
effectively as the artificial particles did in the laboratory, and
in the altostratus cloud described above, are microscopic
soil particles such as clays, loess, and volcanic dust. You
may wonder how scientists can know that these kinds of
particles are likely to trigger ice-crystal growth. The answer

is relatively simple: scientists capture snow crystals, melt them on the stage of a microscope, then search for nuclei and identify them.

Although you would have great difficulty in duplicating the work scientists have done with ice crystals and nuclei, you may like to capture snow crystals and preserve them, either to observe their beauty or to do your own scientific investigation. The steps necessary to produce snow crystal replications are as follows:

(1) Dilute 0.5 to 3% sol. polyvinyl formal (a plastic) dissolved in ethylene dichloride (a common solvent).
(2) Cool a few degrees below 0° C. (32° F.).
(3) Pour onto black cardboard, glass plate, or other flat material that has been cooled to the same temperature.
(4) Hold so that snow falls on the flat surface.
(5) Keep in a cold, well-ventilated place until solvent dries — several minutes.
(6) After solvent dries, take indoors; replications may then be studied.

IV

Thunderstorms

One of the most spectacular, yet common, storms experienced on earth is the thunderstorm. It is estimated that about 44,000 thunderstorms occur each day, primarily in the region from the equator to the arctic circles. Thunderstorms are most frequent in tropical regions, as in equatorial Africa, Panama, and Indonesia. In the United States they are most frequent in Florida (Fig. 1).

Thunderstorms are spawned by cumulonimbus clouds, or thunderheads as they are commonly called. They look like huge, lumpy snow-covered mountains floating in the air (Fig. 2). These gigantic clouds may cause great destruction as they pass overhead. A single thundercloud may have stored within it potential energy comparable to that of several atomic bombs of World War II vintage.

The release of energy from a large thundercloud is awesome. Powerful strokes of lightning flash across the sky, followed by deafening thunderclaps. Although the roar of thunder may be frightening, it is harmless. Lightning, however, shatters trees, starts forest fires, destroys portions of man-made structures, disrupts electrical communications, and can electrocute or burn persons and animals unfortunate enough to be in its path. Also, powerful gusts of wind surging

Annual Thunderstorm Frequency

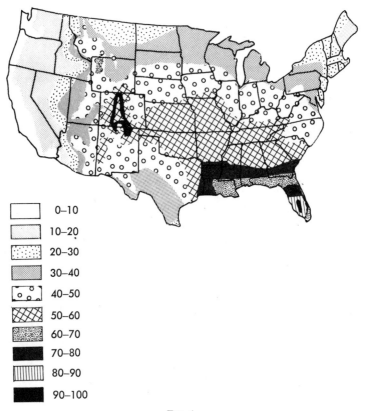

FIG. 1

from thunderclouds may uproot trees, knock down power-lines, rip away rooftops, and capsize small boats. At times, cloudbursts from such clouds release sudden torrents of rain that cause hazardous flooding of streets and highways, farms, and streams. Rampaging streams may wash away homes, bridges, and highways; and smashing hail (Fig. 3) may kill farm animals, strip crops ready for harvest, and damage buildings and vehicles.

Although thunderstorms cause great damage, they are also greatly beneficial to man. Without the moisture of thunderstorms many farms in the Midwest would not be able to produce crops and many communities throughout the country would find their reservoirs going dry. Furthermore, when lightning flashes through the atmosphere it triggers a chemical reaction that causes millions of tons of nitrogen to be washed into the soil each year. This natural fertilizer is used by plants in their growth processes.

Thunderstorm Development

Anyone who has seen fleecy white cumulus clouds forming during warm summer days surely has remarked about their beautiful changing puffed-up forms. Essentially, these clouds are bubbles of warm, moist air that have been heated by contact with the earth's surface, have become lighter, floated upward, and become visible as a result of condensation.

The formation of these clouds depends largely on a relatively high moisture content of the air and a relatively large temperature difference between the air near the ground and the air at higher levels. When air temperature differences are small and the moisture content of the air is low, small cumulus clouds form. Ordinarily, their vertical development is limited to less than a few thousand feet in height and they are short-lived, generally lasting for about 5 to 10 minutes. These clouds do not grow to greater height, since the conditions they need for growth—high humidity and large temperature differences—are not present at higher levels. To understand how small clouds develop into the towering

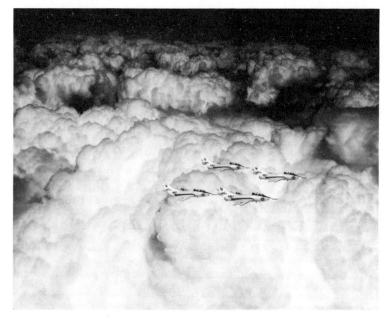

Fig. 2

Fig. 3   *Hail*

cumulonimbus variety, it is necessary to know the physical changes in buoyancy that take place in ascending air, because cumulonimbus clouds, which nurture thunderstorms, develop as a result of the strong uplifting of warm, moist air.

Air Density Affects Uplifting

Important in the understanding of thunderstorm development are the factors that determine the density of air, because the upward ballooning of a parcel of air becomes more pronounced if the density of the rising parcel decreases.

Air may become less dense in a number of ways; among these are heating and the addition of water vapor.

When air is heated, it expands so that the mass of its original volume becomes part of a larger volume. Then, by the formula $D = \frac{m}{v}$, we can see the effect of changing the volume of a mass of air. For example, before heating, 1,000 cubic feet of air (v) weighing 80 pounds (m) has a density of .080 lb./cu. ft. Assume the parcel is heated and increases in volume by 10 percent. Then according to the formula $D = \frac{m}{v}$:

$$D = \frac{80}{1,100} \text{ (the increased volume)}$$
$$D = .073 \text{ lb./cu. ft.}$$

Thus, per cubic foot, the heated parcel of air is about .007 of a pound lighter than the original unheated parcel of air (Fig. 4). Under this condition, the lighter air is subjected to an upward force known as the buoyancy force, which causes it to be displaced upward. The upward force would be equal to the difference in weight between the two parcels of air. Accordingly, the lighter a parcel of air becomes, the greater is the buoyancy force displacing it upward.

Air may also be lightened by the addition of water vapor. Although this may seem strange, we can check this by comparing the molecular weight of dry air with that of water vapor. Dry air has a molecular weight of 29; water vapor has a molecular weight of 18. Thus, when water vapor enters a parcel of dry air it displaces some of the heavier gases, causing the parcel of air to become lighter. The addition of

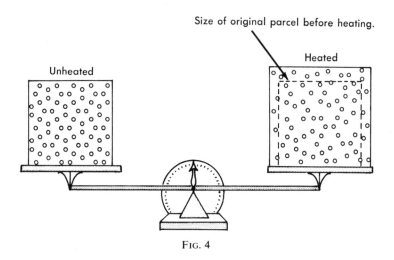

Size of original parcel before heating.

Heated

Unheated

FIG. 4

water vapor has the same effect as raising the temperature of the air. In very dry air, the increase is slight; but when the humidity is high, it has the same effect as raising the air temperature several degrees.

Heat of Vaporization

We saw the initial effect of adding moisture to the air—it lightens the air. The actual presence of moisture, however, is less important than the heat it has acquired in the process of evaporation at the earth's surface. This heat, known as the latent (hidden) heat of vaporization, is stored within the water vapor until it condenses. Upon condensation, each ounce of water vapor has the potential to release about 16,000 calories into the air. When we consider the fact that a large cumulus cloud may contain thousands of tons of water, we can readily see the tremendous amount of heat that has been released in its formation.

As heat is released into a rising mass of air that is undergoing condensation, the cooling rate decreases about 2° to 3° per 1,000 feet of altitude. This cooling rate, based on the condensation of moisture in a rising parcel of air, is called the moist adiabatic rate. Unlike the dry adiabat, which is 5.5° F. per 1,000 feet, the moist adiabat varies according to the amount of water vapor being condensed. Typically, the moist adiabatic rate is about 2° to 3° F. per 1,000 feet of altitude.

Air that becomes lighter because its temperature is higher than the surrounding air will rise until its temperature is that of the surrounding air. Small temperature differences between rising parcels of air and the surrounding air are not sufficient to build large convective clouds, because the rising parcels reach a state of equilibrium too soon. Under such conditions the air is said to be stable. Accordingly, when large temperature differences exist between rising parcels of air and the surrounding environment, the air is described as unstable. This condition favors the formation of cumulonimbus clouds, since parcels of air can be forced upward to greater heights, resulting in clouds of great vertical development. For example, assume a rising parcel of air in which condensation is occurring is cooling at the moist adiabatic rate of 2° per 1,000 feet. By contrast, the lapse rate of the surrounding air is 7° per 1,000 feet. The temperature difference between the rising parcel and the surrounding environment becomes larger as the altitude increases. Under such conditions, the buoyancy force acting on a rising parcel of air becomes greater with increasing height. This results in an increased acceleration of the rising mass of air within the cloud. In effect, the interior of the cloud is like a fireplace chimney in which hot air rises rapidly. And, just as a fire in a fireplace creates a draft in a room by drawing in fresh air to replace air that has been heated and drawn up a chimney, a growing cumulus cloud draws in fresh air from below. As this new air rises, it expands and cools adiabatically, and the moisture within it condenses. If the conditions for rapid uplift — abundant moisture and large temperature differences — still prevail, the chimney will be reinforced and grow higher. The continuous condensation of moisture releases heat within the cloud chimney, thus intensifying the upward current of air. Thus, the cloud continues to grow and attains great vertical development — often extending into the stratosphere.

Thunderstorm Development

Thunderstorms develop in two ways principally — warm, moist air strongly heated by contact with the earth's surface becomes buoyant and is lifted upward, and fronts acting as wedges force warm, moist air upward.

The type of thunderstorms produced by strong heating of the earth's surface usually occur in the summertime (in the afternoon) as the result of the intense heating of the earth's surface by the sun's concentrated rays. These thunderstorms are classified as air-mass thunderstorms; they are also called thermal or convectional thunderstorms.

In the formation of the thermal type of air-mass thunderstorms, warm, moist air typically maritime tropical (mT), in contact with the earth's hot surface, is strongly heated and caused to expand. As a result of expansion, the heated air occupies a larger space. Accordingly, it is lighter, volume for volume, than the surrounding cooler air, especially the air that lies above it. The cooler air, being denser, sinks and displaces the warm air upward. Heating continues, and the warm air is continuously displaced upward by the sinking cool air. This process leads to the growth of thunderstorms.

Thunderstorms caused by the passage of fronts are called frontal thunderstorms. Although they occur throughout the year, they are most numerous during the spring and summer months.

The development of frontal thunderstorms depends upon density differences between air masses. Typically, a continental polar (cP) air mass consisting of cool dry air moves into a region under the influence of maritime tropical (mT) air, which is warm and moist. The leading edge of the dense cP air mass—the cold front—acts as a wedge forcing the less dense mT air upward.

As moist air is lifted upward, as the result of heating, or the wedge action of a front, or of another cause, it remains invisible until condensation occurs. In time, the rising parcels of moist air are cooled to the dew point, condensation occurs, and clouds become visible. The bases of the clouds represent the point at which the air has reached the dew point.

The sequence of events that follows and culminates in thunderstorm activity was little understood until, in 1945, the U.S. Weather Bureau, U.S. Navy, U.S. Air Force, other agencies, and universities cooperated in a venture to make an intensive study of thunderstorms. The venture, which lasted from 1945 to 1950, was called the Thunderstorm Project. It included thousands of penetrations into thunderstorms by means of aircraft and balloons. Before this project, aircraft avoided these storms because it was feared that strong updrafts and downdrafts, lightning, and hail might seriously damage and even destroy planes flying through them. Reports by pilots who were caught in such storms and survived the maelstrom about them led to a healthy respect for thunder-clouds. One navy pilot gives his account of such a storm as follows: "I could not avoid the line of thunderclouds for my fuel was low and the enemy was behind me. As I entered the clouds, the plane was jolted upwards, it bounced around violently, heavy rain and hail smashed against the aircraft, and lightning, flashing about, momentarily blinded me. At one time, according to my air speed indicator, there was no forward motion of my aircraft for a few moments. I had the strange sensation of flying backwards and upwards. As I broke out of the cloud, I checked my altimeter—I was at 8,000 feet. When I entered the cloud I was at 5,000 feet."

Less fortunate were a group of glider pilots who just before World War II attempted to utilize the strong updraft in thunderclouds to carry them to great heights. The turbulence within the clouds was so great that the pilots bailed out—probably believing their gliders would be torn apart. Strong updrafts lifted them to colder higher levels where they were coated with ice. All but one froze to death before they finally dropped out of the cloud.

A remarkable incident of a parachutist surviving an en-counter with a thundercloud occurred in 1959 when the pilot of a military jet, flying at 46,000 feet, had to abandon his plane when the engine flamed out. He fell thousands of feet through a thundercloud before his preset parachute opened auto-matically at 10,000 feet. The sudden jolt of being stopped in free-fall by the blossoming parachute was nothing compared to the harrowing experience that followed. According to the pilot, he was tumbled, spun, shaken, slammed, and pounded violently as lightning flashed about and heavy rain, hail, and snow pelted him. After 45 minutes of being thrown about he dropped out of the cloud and settled to the earth. Fortunately, he wore enough protective gear to limit his injuries to frostbite and slight shock. The full account of this remarkable encounter with a thundercloud can be read in *The Man Who Rode the Thunder* by Lieutenant Colonel William H. Rankin, U.S.M.C. (Prentice-Hall, 1960).

Other tragedies that occurred as a result of encounters with thunderstorms involved lighter-than-air ships known as dirigibles. In the 1920's and 1930's the dirigible was considered by many to be the mode of transportation of the future. (The modern counterpart of the dirigible is the Goodyear blimp commonly seen in various sections of the United States at different times of the year). It is interesting to note this excerpt from an encyclopedia published in 1938: "Dirigible manufacture, however, is moving forward despite tragedies. It is expected that future airships, using helium instead of hydrogen, and correcting the mistakes of former years, will take their places as monarchs of the air."

The tragedies referred to involved a number of lighter-than-air ships. Included among these was the 803-foot-long German passenger dirigible *Hindenburg*. The lift power came from the very light but explosive gas, hydrogen. In 1937 the *Hindenburg*, carrying 93 passengers and crewmen, attempted to land at Lakehurst, New Jersey. Thunderstorms in the area delayed the landing. After the passage of the storms the airship was brought into position for landing. As it hovered 200 feet above the landing site, it suddenly burst into flames. Within a few minutes the ship was completely destroyed. Of the 93 persons aboard, 36 were killed. It is believed that hydrogen leaking from the huge airship was ignited by electricity associated with the thunderstorm activity.

Since hydrogen-filled airships had the potential of being destroyed by fire, the U.S. Navy used helium to fill its airships. Although helium provides less lift, it is inert and does not burn. Yet in 1925 thunderstorms resulted in the destruction of the U.S. Navy's *Shenandoah*. The *Shenandoah*

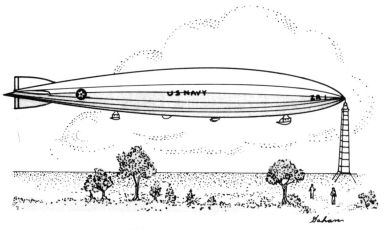

FIG. 5 *The* Shenandoah

(Fig. 5), which was 78 feet long, was caught in a thunderstorm while cruising over Ohio. Caught in strong updrafts and downdrafts, the ship broke into three pieces and fell to earth. Of the 43 men aboard, 14 were killed.

The above accounts, and numerous other incidents involving thunderstorms, demonstrated the need for a better understanding of the forces at work within thunderclouds. Although some information about thunderstorms was compiled from various sources, such as pilots and scientists in mountain observatories, little was known about the dynamics of thunderclouds until the Thunderstorm Project was undertaken. As a result of this project much of the mystery of the forces at work within thunderclouds was eliminated. One important revelation was the discovery that the apparently continuous growth of a thunderstorm could be divided into three stages — the cumulus stage, the mature stage, and the dissipation stage.

The Cumulus Stage

Although the following description of the development of a thunderstorm is typical of the air-mass type it is largely applicable to most thunderstorms.

Thunderstorms have their origin in small cumulus clouds that represent the condensation of moist bubbles of air that have been uplifted and cooled. The cumulus-building stage lasts for about 10 to 15 minutes. During this time the individual cumulus clouds or cells are characterized by vertical updrafts operating within the cloud. Throughout this period the cloud is growing at a rapid pace. The updraft, which is building up the cloud, begins at the ground and continues to the top of the cloud. In the upper portion of the cloud updrafts are the strongest, in the vicinity of 35 miles per hour. Updrafts in the cloud increase as heat is added to the cloud by the condensation of water vapor into cloud particles. Fortified by the added heat, the cloud continues to develop rapidly. Within minutes, a relatively small cumulus cloud, generally a mile or so in diameter and about a mile or two high, grows into a mountainous heap that may be several miles wide and about 5 to 7 miles high. During this growth period the cloud climbs above the freezing level. (Assuming a typical summer day temperature of 85° at the earth's surface, temperatures may be freezing about 3 miles up.) Above the freezing level, small particles of ice and snow crystals join together into larger particles, releasing heat energy in the process. This additional heat helps to sustain the updrafts at higher levels. And as heat is released into the cloud, buoyancy is increased, and the air in the cloud chimney rises more rapidly. Measurements indicate that a parcel of air rising at about 3 miles per hour in the lower levels of a cloud may be accelerated to 60 miles per hour by the time it reaches the top of a 5-mile-high cloud. Throughout the upward swelling cloud, hydrometeors — rain, snow, and hail — are bounced about and kept aloft by the strong currents of upward-swirling air. The suspended particles of rain, snow, and hail increase in size so that it becomes increasingly difficult for updrafts to support them. Eventually, numerous hydrometeors — largely rain and hail — become so heavy that their downward velocity exceeds that of the updrafts, and precipitation begins. The descending precipitation particles drag air within the lower part of the cloud downward, thus creating a downdraft. The beginning of precipitation and downdrafts marks the end of the cumulus stage and the beginning of the mature stage.

The Mature Stage

During the mature stage thunderstorms reach their peak of vertical development, often extending into the stratosphere, which in middle latitudes is about 7 miles up. At times, thunderclouds attain heights of more than 12 miles. Since the top portion of such clouds extends into the upper westerlies, the top of the cloud is flattened by these strong winds, forming the familiar anvil-shaped top.

With the beginning of precipitation, cloud dynamics become more complex, because as precipitation particles fall through the cloud, they tend to evaporate. Since evaporation is a cooling process, the sinking air cools, becomes more dense, and descends more rapidly. In addition, cooler air surrounding the cloud is pulled in (meteorologists call this entrainment) and adds to the density of the cloud air. Thus, the downdrafts are intensified.

The mature stage is characterized by strong updrafts and downdrafts existing side by side, with the descending air occupying the central forward region of the cloud and the ascending air pouring in from the general outer periphery of the cloud. Updraft speeds appear to reach their maximum early in the mature stage. From radar and aircraft observations, and by the calculation of the fall speed of hailstones, updraft speeds are known to exceed a mile a minute, possibly attaining speeds of two to three miles a minute. Downdraft speeds are approximately half these speeds. Ordinarily, aircraft can withstand these strong vertical currents of air. However, sudden choppy gusts accompanying these currents slam against the aircraft with enough force to cause structural damage, thus increasing the hazards of flying through such clouds.

Downdrafts continue to the earth's surface, where they spread horizontally in all directions and are felt as cool, gusty winds. The strongest gusts are felt ahead of the storm, usually in the eastern quadrant. How often have you noticed that, just before a thunderstorm hit, there was a sudden surge of cool air that scattered leaves, papers, and other loose objects about? Prior to this, lighter winds, generally from the south, blew toward the storm. Since gusty winds often extend a mile or two ahead of a storm, it may take a few minutes or so for the thundercloud to appear overhead. As the thundercloud approaches, large raindrops splatter about. At times, hailstones may accompany the drops of rain. Then, when the cloud moves overhead, the precipitation intensifies and the winds generally die down. The most intense precipitation occurs when the central region or core of the cloud is overhead. The heavy precipitation usually lasts from about 5 to 15 minutes, and as the cloud moves ahead, the showers gradually decrease. Thus, from the time the first precipitation particles strike the ground until the end of precipitation, 20 to 30 minutes may have elapsed.

Although thundershowers usually last for less than half an hour, they often deposit as much, or more, precipitation on the ground than the typical warm-front rainstorms that may persist for a day or more. For example, rain occurring during the approach and passage of an extensive warm front may equal an inch or two over 24 hours. A thunderstorm may drop the same amount (or several times more) of precipitation in less than 30 minutes.

At times, updrafts diminish and become too weak to support many of the raindrops being held aloft, and a "cloudburst" results. During a cloudburst a large portion of the water being held aloft is suddenly released. By a person standing beneath the cloud, thick sheets and streams of rain are seen to pour downward. At such times, an inch or more of rain may accumulate in about one minute causing flash floods. Such flash floods can, under certain conditions, cause extensive property damage and result in the drowning of humans and livestock and other animals.

During the mature stage, large electrical charges build up in the cumulonimbus cloud, producing lightning strokes that flash in the sky. The heat created by the surging strokes of electricity produces the thunder that is characteristic of thunderstorms. Lightning and thunder are discussed in greater detail in Chapter V.

In time, the updrafts within the cell die down; eventually the only vertical movement is downward. As the updrafts diminish, the supply of warm, moist air that nurtures the cloud diminishes also, and the mature stage ends.

The Dissipating Stage

Thus with its supply of water vapor cut off, the energy needed to maintain updrafts in the mature cloud diminishes and the cloud enters the final stage. This stage is appropriately called the dissipating stage. Turbulence, rain, thunder, and lightning diminish and then stop altogether as the cloud evaporates rapidly and eventually disperses. However, dissipation does not always mark the end of thunderstorm activity in a locality, as a large thunderstorm may consist of several cells at different stages of development. Accordingly, thunderstorm activity may persist for hours.

Often an advancing cold front has a line of heavy showers and thunderstorms moving well ahead of the cold front. Meteorologists call this pre-cold frontal line of storms squall lines.

Squall lines are believed to be formed by tongues of cold air rushing downward and outward from the cold mass of air associated with the cold front. This onrushing mass of dense air scoops up warm air many miles—generally up to 150 miles—ahead of the front, triggering heavy showers and thunderstorms. Strong gusts, at times of hurricane force (74 mph and higher), occur in squalls.

V

Lightning and Thunder

Of all of nature's phenomena, thunder and lightning are probably the most dramatic. In ancient times thunder and lightning were thought to represent the unleashing of the power and wrath of gods. To this day the symbolism of thunder and lightning is deeply ingrained in much of our literature, especially in horror movies. One of the best examples of this is the utilization of lightning to kindle "life" in the Frankenstein monster.

In real life, some men tried to explain the nature of lightning by observing it and trying to duplicate it. Almost every student has heard of Benjamin Franklin's famous kite-flying experiment during a thunderstorm. Previous to this, Franklin had done many experiments with electricity. One of his noted contributions was the concept that lightning is a single "fluid" and that opposite charges (negative and positive) simply represent different levels of one kind of electricity.

Franklin noted, as did others, that tall objects—spires, trees, chimneys, hilltops—attracted lightning. From his observations he speculated that lightning could be safely drawn from a cloud by means of a long rod of iron placed on top of buildings or masts of ships. He soon realized the need for a ground wire to direct the lightning safely away from buildings or ships. Soon lightning rods became commonplace.

Although Franklin's lightning rods were usually effective in diverting lightning away from structures, there have been occasions when lightning hits have destroyed buildings protected by rods (Fig. 1). One of the more spectacular and

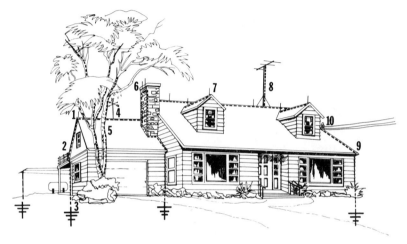

FIG. 1   *Lightning protection points for a house: 1) terminals spaced a minimum of 20 feet apart along ridges and within 2 feet of ridge ends; 2) downlead conductors; 3) at least two grounds, at least 10 feet deep, for house—additional grounds for clotheslines, etc.; 4) roof projections such as ornaments tied into conductor system; 5) protection for tree within 10 feet of house—connect to house grounding; 6) at least two terminals on chimneys; 7) dormers rodded; 8) arrester on antenna—connect to main conductor; 9) tie-in to conductor system of gutter within 6 feet of conductor; 10) arrester on overhead power lines.*

tragic examples of such an occurrence took place in the summer of 1926, when lightning struck a huge ammunition dump in New Jersey. Even though the ammunition storage buildings were protected with lightning rods, a lightning discharge ignited one of the magazines (storage units). The explosions that followed destroyed all buildings within about a half mile.

Chunks of debris were propelled as far as 22 miles. Sixteen people were killed, and $70,000,000 dollars worth of property was destroyed.

Although scientists cannot fully explain how a thundercloud produces lightning, they know a great deal about the nature of charges in thunderclouds. According to observations, thunderclouds contain areas in which negative charges and positive charges are concentrated. In the idealized thundercloud (Fig. 2a), the top and bottom of the cloud have a concentration of positive charges and the middle of the cloud is negatively charged. In nature, the charges are probably more like those shown in Fig. 2b.

The charges in thunderclouds may be the result of friction and collisions between cloud particles, air, ions, and other bits of matter in clouds. This concept is substantiated by the fact that wind-blown dust, or other particles, and smoking volcanoes can be electrically charged. Another possibility is that the breaking apart of raindrops may produce different charges. This may be compared to the charges generated when one removes a sweater made of a synthetic fabric. Other possible sources of cloud charges are charged particles carried by upcurrents and downcurrents in clouds, or raindrops that become charged by induction when small droplets collide with large drops and lose electrons to the large drops. In the latter instance, the heavier drops would carry strong negative charges downward, leaving the strongly positive charged droplets higher up in the cloud.

Whatever the cause, the charges that have built up in the base of a thundercloud are matched by an opposite charge on the surface of the earth. When the charge becomes strong enough to jump the gap between the cloud and the ground, or between clouds, or within the cloud itself, electrons stream across the gap, producing the lightning flash. Since the elec-

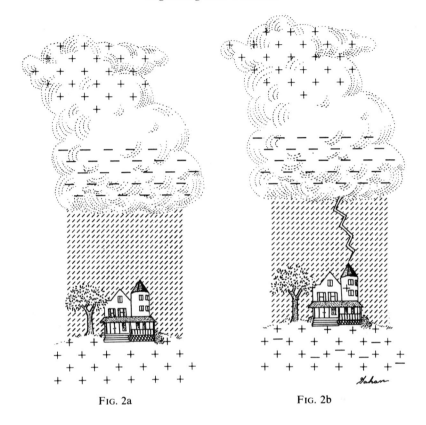

FIG. 2a   FIG. 2b

trons flow most readily across small gaps, high objects become "targets" for lightning discharges.

Favorite Lightning Targets

Because high objects are favorite targets of lightning discharges, it is a good idea to stay away from hills and large trees during thunderstorms. According to this rule, we would expect mountainous regions to be extremely dangerous; yet mountain peaks above 18,000 feet are largely free of lightning strokes. Studies indicate that with increasing altitude lightning discharges tend to occur at lower voltages and involve lower currents. For example, measurements of a power line crossing the Rocky Mountains indicate that it was struck by lightning 145 times over a period of four years. Currents for the parts of the line at lower altitudes were higher than the currents recorded at higher altitudes. Although lower currents are more prevalent at higher altitudes, this does not necessarily imply that the hazards of lightning are greatly diminished. For example, in one section of the Rockies, foresters report twice as many fires produced by lightning at altitudes of about 1 $\frac{1}{2}$ miles as at altitudes of about $\frac{1}{2}$ mile.

At times, there may be a large enough gap between the electrically charged upper portions of a thundercloud and a mountain peak for lightning discharges to occur (Fig. 3a). Interestingly, when mountains extend into thunderclouds the charge in these clouds leaks away gradually and the lightning hazard is greatly reduced. Usually the electric charge leaks away harmlessly (Fig. 3b).

Whatever the nature of the terrain, trees are most vulnerable to lightning strokes. Because trees contain large amounts of moisture, they provide easy paths for electrons to travel along. Thus, the moisture content of a tree makes it a relatively good conductor of electricity. For example, a live tree may conduct electricity hundreds of thousands of times better than a dead tree containing little or no moisture. The moisture content of trees is higher in the summer than in the winter, thus trees are more vulnerable to lightning in the warmer months.

The type of tree most likely to be struck by lightning depends on a number of factors. Tall trees, of course, are

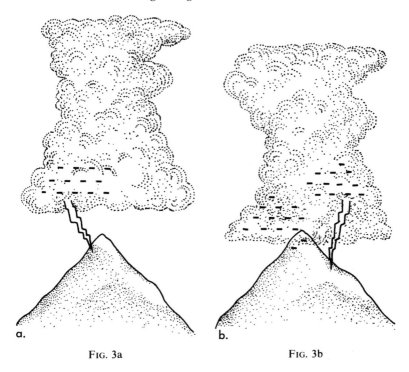

FIG. 3a   FIG. 3b

prime targets (Fig. 4). The oak tree seems to attract lightning more than others. In folklore, the oak is often referred to as a lightning attracter. In one adage from folklore, the danger of standing beneath oak trees during lightning storms is pointedly stated: "Beware an oak: it draws the stroke." Because oak trees were obvious targets of lightning strokes, the wood of oak trees became an object of superstition in early societies. As recently as the mid-nineteenth century, oak logs were believed to be related to supernatural powers, since oak trees seemed to be singled out for lightning hits from the heavens. Some day, after much more research, we

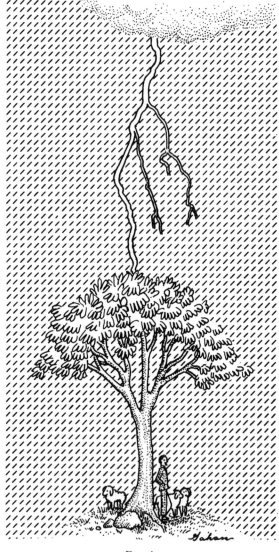

FIG. 4

may find that in stands of trees where no trees dominate in height, the most important lightning-hit factors will be the moisture content of the trees. The research may support the old superstitions, for oaks are known to have a higher moisture content than most other trees.

When lightning hits a tree, several things can happen—the tree may start to burn, the trunk may explode, bark may be stripped loose, or the charge may travel to the ground with little or no effect. The degree and type of damage depend on a number of factors, including the strength of the lightning stroke, the type of lightning stroke, the type of tree struck, and the moisture condition of the tree. Although the effects of lightning on trees differ, observers have found that oaks tend to explode frequently. This may be because the inner region of the oak contains much moisture. The water, heated by the tremendous surge of electricity through the trunk, probably expands rapidly, changes to steam, and shatters the trunk explosively. Of course, powerful lightning strokes can cause other kinds of objects to explode violently. In the spring of 1966 a lightning bolt struck a 1-foot-thick brick wall (a parapet) on the roof of a school building in which I worked. A section of the wall about 9 feet long by 4 feet deep was destroyed. The explosion was so great that whole bricks were blasted over a high cyclone-type fence for more than 150 feet.

The Physical Nature of Lightning Bolts

Strange as it may seem, there is hot and cold lightning. Since all lightning strokes are quite hot, the term cold is relative. Temperatures of 27,000 degrees Fahrenheit and even higher have been measured—about three times hotter than the sun's visible surface.

Hot lightning tends to start fires, whereas cold lightning tends to have explosive effects. These greatly different effects can be explained by their nature: hot lightning has relatively low currents that last a long time; cold lightning has very high currents that last a very short time. In general, hot lightning lasts from 20 to 100 times longer than cold lightning. Since the duration of a typical lightning flash is measured in hundredths of a second (the luminous flash persists for a second or so), both hot and cold bolts discharge in far less time than it would take to blink your eyes. A cold bolt, then, ordinarily releases its energy so quickly that an explosion occurs before a fire can even be started in the struck material.

Fulgurites

Would you believe that there is such a thing as petrified lightning! You may have even come across a section or remnant of petrified lightning without being aware of its nature. If you have ever stumbled on such a substance you may have thought it was formed by a burrowing animal that had lined its hole or burrow with cemented sand particles. That is about what petrified lightning looks like — a hollow tube of cemented sand. Scientists call these tubes fulgurites from the Latin word for lightning, *fulgur.*

Fulgurites form when lightning strikes sandy places such as beaches. As the lightning surges into the ground, the searing heat melts sand particles in its path, causing them to fuse together and form glass. Sand particles fused to the glass give the glass a coarse appearance. These glass tubes are hollow and shaped like uneven rods or tree branches. Most fulgurites that have been discovered range from about $\frac{1}{4}$ inch to 3 inches in diameter. One of the largest fulgurites found was about 9 feet long, and the glass walls were about the thickness of several sheets of notebook paper. Since fulgurites have been found in all parts of the United States, it may interest you to search sandy areas *after* thunderstorms have passed through. You may find a fulgurite, one of nature's rarest and strangest treasures. Digging up your find may create a frustrating problem, because fulgurites are relatively fragile. If you proceed with extreme caution, however, you may manage to remove a large section of the fulgurite in one piece.

Streak Lightning

The type of lightning discharge we are most familiar with is called streak lightning. This is the kind we usually draw when we want to depict a lightning stroke. We draw it as a zigzag streak. Actual photographs of streak lightning, however, show that it follows a twisting course through the air. This path is prepared by electrons streaming between a cloud and the ground. Surprisingly, the path the electrons follow is not necessarily the shortest distance between the cloud and the ground. The moving electrons ionize the air, causing it to become a good conductor of electricity. Additional electrons then surge downward, "zigzagging" along the ionized path, and rush toward the ground at speeds in the neighborhood of 200,000 feet per second. The electrons flow downward in steps, pausing periodically (typically every 150 feet) for brief moments measured in millionths of a second; then they surge onward. As they approach the earth, another stream of electrons flows upward along an ionized path that develops from the ground. When the streams of electrons meet, the cloud and the ground are connected as if by an invisible electric wire. Then, electrons pour downward toward the earth, which has already had a positive charge induced in it by the base of the negatively charged cloud. The entire process produces a weakly lighted but highly conductive path called the leader. Then a great surge of electrons rushing through the leader induces a return stroke which produces the brilliant flash that we see in the sky as lightning. Photographs of lightning indicate that the return stroke begins at the base of the ionized leader and proceeds upward. The upward movement is so fast that the return stroke appears to light up the channel all at once. Other strokes, about three or four, may follow at intervals of a few thousandths of seconds. As many as 40 strokes may be part of one lightning flash. A typical stroke produces currents of about 30,000 amperes; some strokes may be as high as 345,000 amperes. (In terms of home usage, a 100-watt bulb operates on less than 1 ampere.)

The tremendous outpouring of electrons in a lightning stroke leaves a weakly charged condition between the cloud and the earth. Usually, in about 20 seconds a strong charge builds up again between the cloud and the earth and once more the stage is set for another lightning discharge.

The tremendous surge of electrons in a lightning stroke raises the air temperature in the channel several thousand degrees within a split second. This sudden heating causes a violent expansion of the air, which produces intense sound waves heard as thunder. Lightning and its accompanying thunder are not detected at the same moment because the flash of lightning and the sound of thunder travel at greatly different speeds. Light travels at about 186,000 miles per second, whereas sound waves travel about 1000 feet per second. Thus, when a lightning flash occurs, the light is seen instantaneously. The thunder that is produced at the same moment is heard immediately only when lightning strikes close by. As the distance increases, the time it takes for thunder to be heard also increases. Thus, when we consider the speed of sound waves at 1000 feet per second, a lapse of five seconds between a lightning flash and thunder indicates the lightning is about one mile away. Next time there is a thunderstorm in your vicinity, try estimating the distance of the storm by counting the seconds between the lightning flash and the thunder. For each second, add 1000 feet of distance. In most cases, thunder will be heard in much less than one minute after the flash.

You may have noticed different kinds of thunder; typically there is the rumbling type and the sudden sharp, snapping type. The differences in these sounds are attributed to the nature of sound waves and the distance between the observer and the thunder source. Sound waves of short length have high frequencies that produce sharp, whipping noises. Conversely, low-frequency sound waves produce dull, rumbling noises. Because short waves are quickly absorbed by the atmosphere, they do not travel as far as do longer waves, which are not readily absorbed. Thus, observers near a lightning flash hear sharp, cracking noises that may be described as bangs, or like snaps of a whip; distant observers hear rumbling noises. If you ever hear a loud, crackling blast, the lightning discharge is probably close by — within about 150 feet of you. Rumbling is also caused by small differences in travel time for lightning strokes that occur in scattered sections of a cloud at the same time.

Often the familiar streak lightning may produce branches that appear to stab at the ground. This type of lightning is often referred to as forked lightning.

At times we may also see flashes of lightning that appear as heads, ribbons, sheets, or even balls.

Bead Lightning

Bead lightning, also called chain lightning, appears as blobs of light of varying intensities strung together. The separated blobs may be the result of the disintegration of ordinary streak lightning. Possibly, the distinct flashes of light may not exist — they may be optical illusions or other distortions that appear to observers as beads of light all in a row.

Ribbon Lightning

Ribbon lightning is produced when strong winds push the ionized channel sideways. As a result, consecutive strokes move through channels that run parallel to each other. Since consecutive strokes may follow each other at intervals measured in hundredths or thousandths of a second — and the eye retains images for about $1/10$ of a second — the series of strokes are seen at the same time. This appears as a band or ribbon of long irregular streaks of light of varying intensities.

Heat Lightning

At times you may have seen distant lightning flashes that could not be heard. Or you may have seen flashes of light without actually seeing lightning strokes. This type of lightning is called heat lightning. It is not different from ordinary lightning; it is just too far away for us to observe its full intensity. Most thunder is heard within a range of about 9 miles. Under ideal conditions, topography being an important factor, thunder may be heard from as far as 18 miles. Usually, however, the sound of thunder dissipates and becomes inaudible when it comes from a lightning discharge 10 or more miles away.

Sheet Lightning

Sheet lightning is seen as wide expanses of whitish light glowing in and around a cloud. The glow tends to persist for a relatively long time as compared to streak lightning. Nevertheless, as in the case of heat lightning, sheet lightning is really ordinary lightning. It appears as a sheet of light because the lightning flashes are obscured by clouds and show up only as pulsating sheets of light.

Lightning Balls

The strangest of all forms of lightning is ball lightning. Although many people claim to have observed ball lightning, there is much controversy about its actual existence. Some scientists believe it may be an optical illusion. Yet from studies of many reports, we have a pretty good idea of what ball lightning looks like – if it exists! Various observers have described ball lightning as a round blob of reddish-yellow or bluish-white light moving at speeds of up to hundreds of feet per second. These balls, which may be several inches or more in diameter, have been reported traveling along fences, sliding down trees, drifting through hallways, and even popping through keyholes. Although most who encounter these strange "fire-balls" escape unharmed, there have been reports of injuries such as slight burns and some shock.

From data compiled in the laboratory, and from the reports of observers, scientists believe lightning balls may be concentrations of highly charged particles in the atmosphere with temperatures of several thousands of degrees. The cause of their movement may be the wind, or air currents, or attraction by the earth's magnetic field, or attraction by opposing charges nearby. Possibly, lightning balls are mere optical illusions caused by the dazzling effect produced by a brilliant flash of lightning.

St. Elmo's Fire

At times, when thunderstorms are overhead, a bluish glow may be seen flickering around exposed objects such as lightning rods, steeples, flagpoles, ship masts, tree branches, chimneys, the corners of houses, and even around various points on aircraft. At night this strange flamelike glow produces eerie effects as it flickers about. The glow is caused by electrical discharges from various points on objects.

In the days of sailing ships, the weird glow appearing on the masts and rigging of ships led Mediterranean sailors to name the phenomenon St. Elmo's (Erasmus) Fire, after their patron saint.

Ordinarily St. Elmo's fire is harmless. It is believed, however, that the Hindenburg (a huge dirigible filled with hydrogen gas) was destroyed (May 6, 1937, at Lakehurst, N.J.) when electrical discharges on its skin ignited gases escaping from one of the airship's gas containers.

If you ever see St. Elmo's fire nearby, you will probably hear a crackling noise accompanying it. This crackling noise is produced by the discharge of electricity along various points. The appearance of St. Elmo's fire indicates that a lightning discharge is imminent. Under such conditions it is wise to take precautions to avoid injury. Even if St. Elmo's fire is not occurring, if thunderstorms are in your vicinity, it is a good idea to protect your life and property by observing the standard safety rules for thunderstorms.

LIGHTNING SAFETY RULES

These safety rules will help you save your life when lightning threatens:

(1) **Stay indoors,** and don't venture outside, unless absolutely necessary.

(2) **Stay away from open doors and windows,** fireplaces, radiators, stoves, metal pipes, sinks, and plug-in electrical appliances.

(3) **Don't use plug-in electrical equipment** such as hair dryers, electric toothbrushes, or electric razors during the storm.

(4) **Don't use the telephone during the storm** — lightning may strike telephone lines outside.

(5) **Don't take laundry off the clothesline.**

(6) **Don't work on fences,** telephone or power lines, pipelines, or structural steel fabrication.

(7) **Don't use metal objects** such as fishing rods and golf clubs. Golfers wearing cleated shoes are particularly good lightning rods.

(8) **Don't handle flammable materials** in open containers.

(9) **Stop tractor work,** especially when the tractor is pulling metal equipment, and dismount. Tractors and other implements in metallic contact with the ground are often struck by lightning.

(10) **Get out of water** and off small boats.

(11) **Stay in your automobile** if you are traveling. Automobiles offer excellent lightning protection.

(12) **Seek shelter in buildings.** If no buildings are available, your best protection is a cave, ditch, canyon, or under head-high clumps of trees in open forest glades.

(13) **When there is no shelter,** avoid the highest object in the area. If only isolated trees are nearby, your best protec-

tion is to crouch in the open, keeping twice as far away from isolated trees as the trees are high.

(14) **Avoid hill tops,** open spaces, wire fences, metal clotheslines, exposed sheds, and any electrically conductive elevated objects.

(15) **When you feel the electrical charge** — if your hair stands on end or your skin tingles — lightning may be about to strike you. Drop to the ground immediately.

Persons struck by lightning receive a severe electrical shock and may be burned, but they carry no electrical charge and can be handled safely. A person "killed" by lightning can often be revived by prompt mouth-to-mouth resuscitation, cardiac massage, and prolonged artificial respiration. In a group struck by lightning, the apparently dead should be treated first; those who show vital signs will probably recover spontaneously, although burns and other injuries may require treatment. Recovery from lightning strikes is usually complete except for possible impairment or loss of sight or hearing.*

THUNDERSTORM SAFETY RULES

(1) **Keep an eye on the weather** during warm periods and during the passage of cold fronts. When cumulus clouds begin building up and darkening, you are probably in for a thunderstorm. Check the latest weather forecast.

(2) **Keep calm.** Thunderstorms are usually of short duration; even squall lines pass in a matter of a few hours. Be cautious, but don't be afraid. Stay indoors and keep informed.

---

* Taussig, H. B., "Death From Lightning — and the Possibility of Living Again," *Annals of Internal Medicine,* Vol. 68, No. 6, June 1968.

(3) **Know what the storm is doing.** Remember that the mature stage may be marked on the ground by a sudden reversal of wind direction, a noticeable rise in wind speed, and a sharp drop in temperature. Heavy rain, hail, tornadoes, and lightning generally occur only in the mature stage of the thunderstorm.

(4) **Conditions may favor tornado formation.** Tune in your radio or television receiver to determine whether there is a tornado watch or tornado warning out for your area. *A tornado watch* means tornado formation is likely in the area covered by the watch. *A tornado warning* means one has been sighted or radar-indicated in your area. *If you receive a tornado warning,* seek inside shelter in a storm cellar, below ground level, or in reinforced concrete structures; stay away from windows.

(5) **Lightning** is the thunderstorm's worst killer. Stay indoors and away from electrical appliances while the storm is overhead. If lightning catches you outside, remember that it seeks the easiest — not necessarily the shortest — distance between positive and negative centers. Keep yourself lower than the nearest highly conductive object, and maintain a safe distance from it. If the object is a tree, twice its height is considered a safe distance.

(6) **Thunderstorm rain** may produce flash floods. Stay out of dry creek beds during thunderstorms. If you live along a river, listen for flash-flood warnings from the National Weather Service.

VI

Tornadoes

This simulated "Tornado Watch Bulletin" is typical of
the first warning issued by a Forecast Center of the National
Weather Service when conditions over a region indicate that
tornadoes are expected to develop. During this period,
persons in the "watch" area—usually 140 miles wide by
240 miles long—are instructed to continue their normal
routines but to watch for threatening weather and to listen
to radio and TV broadcasts for further information.

When a severe thunderstorm or tornado is actually sighted,

88

or detected by radar, a "Tornado Warning Bulletin" is issued. Then the Weather Service indicates the location of the tornado or thunderstorm, the time period, and the specific areas that could be affected. For example:

TORNADO REPORTED 5 MILES WEST OF POTOSI AT 7 PM CDT. — MOVING TOWARD THE EAST AT 30 TO 35 MPH.

When a warning is received, immediate action is necessary, as it may mean life or death. Thus, all persons close to the storm should take cover immediately. Those farther away should be prepared to act as soon as threatening conditions are sighted. It is especially important for those in a tornado watch area to keep an eye on the sky, since tornadoes often come and go so quickly that there may be little or no time to act. At times, a tornado cloud with its characteristic funnel twisting back and forth may be clearly visible for several miles. Sometimes the funnel may be obscured by ragged scud clouds extending to the ground. At other times, the funnel may suddenly descend from a storm cloud and reach toward the earth. The bottoms of such clouds have a strange bumpy appearance that may be compared to numerous black cow udders suspended from the base of the cloud (Fig. 1). Appropriately, the name given these protuberances is mammatocumulus — "mamma" relating to the milk-producing structures in female mammals.

Forces at Work in Tornadoes

Wherever a tornado funnel touches the earth, total destruction ordinarily occurs, as the funnel contains extremely low air pressure and whirling winds of 200 to 500 miles per hour — or higher! The combination of extremely low pressure and high velocity winds is deadly. As tornado winds hammer at the exterior of a house, the air inside the house presses outward into the extremely low pressure region inside the funnel. Since the typical tornado usually moves at more than

FIG. 1   *Mammato Cumulus Clouds*

30 miles per hour, it can appear over a house quite suddenly — which results in a rapid pressure drop in the air surrounding the building. Thus, the air pressure within the house is suddenly much greater than the outside air pressure (Fig. 2A). Whereas moments earlier the pressure inside was equal to the outside pressure, the inside pressure may now be 10 percent higher — or the equivalent of about two extra pounds

of outward thrust per square inch. In a one-story house, with dimensions of about 20 feet wide and 30 feet deep, the outward push on the four outer walls and the ceiling would be about 450,000 pounds or more. If the doors and windows

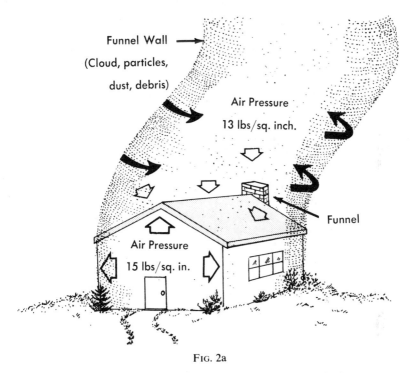

Funnel Wall

(Cloud, particles,

dust, debris)

Air Pressure

13 lbs/sq. inch.

Air Pressure

15 lbs/sq. in.

Funnel

FIG. 2a

are closed, the inside air, having no easy outlet, expands outward suddenly as if an explosion had occurred inside the building. Thus, windows explode, walls burst outward, and rooftops are lifted (Fig. 2B). Simultaneously, winds of hundreds of miles per hour may slam into the exploding house and add to the demolition of its parts. The high winds scatter assorted debris — metal, glass, wood, bricks — throughout the

area. These objects, driven at great speeds, become dangerous death-dealing missiles. The force with which they smash
into objects is unbelievable — small particles are like shotgun
pellets; ordinary brittle straws have been driven into telephone poles, trees, and the walls of wooden buildings.

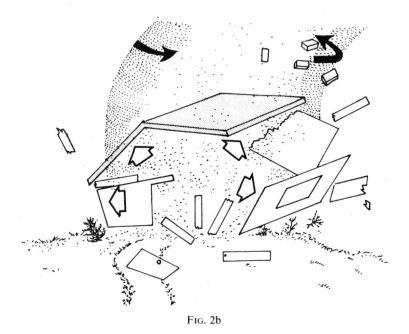

FIG. 2b

One tornado sheared the wool off a herd of sheep. Another carried a herd of cattle through the air. There are
numerous accounts of other strange effects caused by tornadoes. One tornado pulled the water out of a river (West
Fork River, W.Va.) and left it temporarily dry. Another
tornado picked up a locomotive, turned it around, and set
it down on another track. And moving passenger trains have
been lifted into the air and dropped many feet away from the

tracks. In other tornadoes, people have been lifted up and carried over rooftops and set down unharmed hundreds of feet away. Blankets have been lifted off people in bed without affecting them. One man reported that when he opened his front door he was sucked up by a tornado and carried about 200 feet through the air. Even more freakish are accounts of fragile objects such as jars of food and mirrors being carried for miles and then set down without breaking. Probably the strangest incident of all happened to a rooster — it was forced into a narrow-necked two-gallon jug without any injury.

When tornadoes rip through residential areas, there is often loss of life. On the average, about 120 persons are likely to be killed each year (Fig. 3). However, statistics can be misleading. For example, from 1958 to 1964, the maximum tornado-related deaths in any one year was 73 (1964). And from 1953 through 1969, in only five years — 1953, 1955, 1957, 1965, 1969 — out of the 17 years, did the death toll exceed 120. Some of the worst tornado disasters are listed below.

SOME TORNADO DISASTERS — 1884 TO 1970

Date	Killed	Comments
Feb. 19, 1884	800	About 60 tornadoes, scattered throughout Alabama, Mississippi, Tennessee, Kentucky, Indiana, and the Carolinas.
May 27, 1896	306	Relatively weak and short-lived tornado; path through St. Louis, Mo.; damage $13,000,000.
March 18, 1925	689	Single tornado; path about 219 miles long, from southeast Missouri through Illinois to Indiana; about $17,000,000 damage; 1,980 injured; known as the Tri-State Tornado.
April 5, 1936	216	Single tornado; path about 20 miles long, part through Tupelo, Miss.; $13,000,000 damage; 700 injured.

Deaths from Tornados 1953–1971*

* Hawaii and Alaska 0

FIG. 3

Date	Killed	Comments
June 23, 1944	153	Four tornadoes; path through mountains of West Virginia and Maryland and into Pennsylvania. Damage $5,000,000.
March 21, 1952 and March 22, 1952	208	31 tornadoes, scattered throughout Alabama, Arkansas, Kentucky, Mississippi, Missouri, Tennessee; damage $14,000,000; about 1,154 injured.
April 11, 1965	271	37 tornadoes struck Illinois, Indiana, Iowa, Michigan, Ohio, Wisconsin; damage $300,000,-000; about 5,000 injured.
May 11, 1970	27	Single tornado, path 8½ miles long, moved through Lubbock, Kansas; 1,040 dwellings destroyed, 8,876 damaged; damage over $125,000,-000; 1,500 injured.

Although the destructive work of tornadoes is quite obvious, many questions concerning tornadoes are yet to be answered. Some questions asked are: how are tornadoes generated, where does their tremendous energy come from, what determines their path and rate of movement, and where are they most likely to strike?

Formation of Tornadoes

At one time or another, every state in the United States has been struck by a tornado. Although tornadoes occur in many countries, they are a phenomenon primarily restricted to North America and Australia. In the United States, most tornadoes (also called twisters and cyclones locally) occur in the Midwest region in the late spring or early summer. However, no time of the year is free of these storms. Most tornadoes occur between noon and midnight. Within this time period, most tornadoes (about 23 percent) occur between 4 P.M. and 6 P.M.

In Figure 3, it is interesting to note that tornado deaths in the Far Western states have been at zero, or near zero, over a 16-year period. These low figures are attributed to two reasons: the Far Western states have either low population densities or few tornadoes, or both (see Fig. 4). As can be seen, there is a large increase in tornado incidence between the Rocky Mountains and the East Coast. Since the population densities are often quite high throughout this region, there is a rather high probability of tornado casualties in the eastern half of the United States.

Many theories have been proposed to explain how tornadoes are born. Although none has been fully accepted by scientists, it is known that tornadoes usually form when the air is warm and humid and severe thunderstorm activity is in progress.

The fact that tornadoes are usually associated with severe thunderstorms indicates that wherever air masses of strongly contrasting temperatures and humidity clash, tornadoes may occur. The importance of temperature differences is demonstrated by the fact that 23 percent of these storms occur

Tornado Incidence by State 1953–1971*

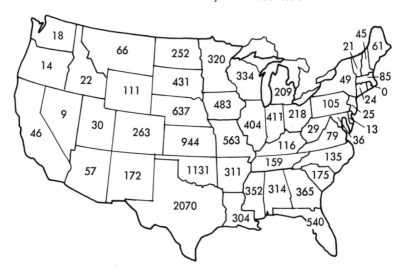

* Alaska 1, Hawaii 9

FIG. 4

between 4 P.M. and 6 P.M.—the time of the day when air temperatures are usually at their highest.

In the spring and summer especially, lines of thunderstorms form along the frontal surface (cold front) of large, cool, dry masses of air pushing generally south and eastward and clashing with warm, moist air masses moving up from the

South. During these months there are often large differences in temperature and humidity between these two opposing air masses. And when there are large differences between opposing air masses, uplifting of the lesser air mass is very strong and rapid.

As a cold air mass advances, friction tends to hold back the surface air, and the higher "friction-free" air spills over and ahead of the thunderstorm line. This cold, dry air spilling on top of the warm, moist air causes the air several miles ahead of the cold front to become highly unstable, or top-heavy. Thus, lines of thunderstorms extending hundreds of miles precede the advancing main mass of air. Weathermen call these lines squall lines. In the Great Plains region the maximum frequency of hail and tornadoes occurs within squall lines.

It is believed that a combination of factors is needed to produce tornadoes. The most important factors appear to be of a thermal and mechanical nature.

The necessary thermal forces are produced when cold air overrides warm air. This condition is most common in the Great Plains region of the United States during the spring and early summer. During these months layers of cool, dry air moving generally south and eastward from the Rocky Mountains region ride over warm, moist surface air moving up from the Gulf of Mexico or the Caribbean. Ordinarily, cool air displaces warm air upward. However, the cool air that has passed over the mountains has been lifted mechanically (orographic uplift), and when it passes over the mountains it sinks downward and warms by compression in its lower levels and becomes very dry. Thus, the overriding mountain air forms a deep layer of dry air, the bottom of which is quite warm. Overall then, a layer of warm, moist air is overlaid by a layer of warm, dry air upon which a layer

of cold, dry air lies. Under this condition a temperature inversion exists at the general boundary between the warm,
moist surface air and the overriding mountain air. This tends
to act as a lid on the warm, moist surface air. Under this
condition the atmosphere is quite stable and convection is
inhibited. Scientists speculate that swift currents of air at
high altitudes—the jet stream—sweeping across the Plains
region from the Southwest are an important factor in triggering tornadoes (Fig. 5). According to some scientists, the jet
stream speeding along at about 15,000 feet has ripples in it
like those in a jump rope when it is snapped. These ripples
create disturbances in the warm, moist air, causing large
sections to be lifted. Probably the rapidly moving jet stream
acts as a pump and pulls the warm, moist air upward and then
carries it away rapidly. The uplifting of large parcels of air
results in great instability, and thunderstorms result. Some of
these thunderstorms may become tornadoes. Weathermen
have found that prior to the development of tornadoes, lines
of thunderstorms usually form parallel to the jet stream. It is
believed by some scientists that lower north-blowing winds
in general opposition to the jet stream work in combination
with the jet stream to add a twisting motion to the rapidly
rising air in the thunderstorm cells. And with an additional
assist from the rotating earth, the air currents swirl rapidly
in small, tight circles. Within this system, heat energy is
continuously released as upward-moving moist air condenses
into cloud droplets. The release of heat intensifies the upward
movement of air. As the air at lower levels swirls upward, it
is rapidly replaced at the lower levels by inward-moving air.
As this inward-moving air moves closer to the point of uplift,
it rotates more and more rapidly. The effect is similar to a
"spinning" ice skater who increases his speed of rotation by
bringing his outstretched arms close to his body. In effect

The Jet Stream as a Factor in Tornado Formation

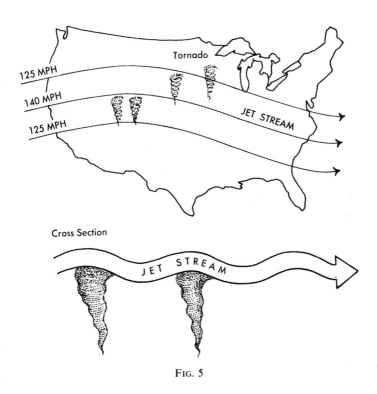

FIG. 5

then, the converging winds accelerate rapidly to tornado velocities.

Some scientists have suggested that lightning or other electrical discharges may play an important part in tornado formation. Many eyewitness reports of lightning associated with tornadoes indicate that it is more intense, much brighter, and more frequent than in thunderstorms. One eyewitness to a tornado in Alabama stated that the "lightning flashes were extremely bright and bluer than I have ever seen—they followed so closely together that the result was a steady illumination which provided more than enough light to read a newspaper in my darkened room."

Of course, the powerful strokes of lightning associated with tornadoes may be produced by the tremendous forces at work within these monster clouds. Many more observations and studies must be made by scientists to begin to understand the processes involved in tornado formation; they may even explain the strange electrical phenomena associated with tornadoes. One great problem for scientists, of course, is how to measure these violent storms by means of instruments, since tornadoes usually form suddenly, move rapidly, and destroy nearly everything they come in contact with. In my years as a weatherman (World War II), I found no one who was either willing to "tangle" with a tornado or who could devise a method to measure them carefully by means of instruments.

Characteristics of Tornadoes

Because of the nature of tornadoes, there have been several instances when people have suddenly found themselves very close to, and even inside, the whirling funnel. In some instances, occupants of houses have had their houses torn apart about them without any serious injury being inflicted upon them. As they watched the churning maelstrom all around, they observed various eerie effects from their positions within the funnel. A Kansas farmer reported seeing his cast-iron stove circling about over his head. In the same incident, his daughter had all her clothes ripped off her body but was unharmed. Other observers have seen farm implements whirling about over their heads. An observer in

Alabama stated that "although the tornado was not directly overhead, our house was lifted up and down at least a half dozen times. My guess is the house rose about six inches off its foundation." [Possibly a similar experience led the author of the *Wizard of Oz* to use a "twister" to transport Dorothy to the land of Oz.] "During the same storm my uncle's house was torn to pieces. His wife was killed. He does not know how he survived. All he can recall is a tremendous roar; very shortly after, less than one minute, he found himself walking two to three blocks away from his house. The storm probably carried him about 500 feet through the air. . . . The power of the storm really amazed me when I was shown a wedge-shaped wood splinter, about one foot long and pencil-thick, that had completely penetrated the trunk of a small tree."

According to other witnesses, tornado funnels have circular openings at their centers that extend upward from hundreds to thousands of feet. Usually the whirling motion within the funnel cloud is in a counterclockwise direction. When within the funnel cavity, observers have noted the rapid lightning flashes similar to those observed by the Alabaman described earlier, who read a newspaper by the steady light. Actual counts of such strokes indicate that lightning flashes occur with machine-gun rapidity—as often as 10 to 20 per second.

The noise associated with tornadoes has been described as sounding like the roar of "50 jets flying right overhead"; "the roar of several freight trains passing right through your house"; "like being surrounded by thousands of roaring cannons." These descriptions may sound exaggerated; however, it is known that the roar of a tornado can be heard 25 miles away.

A sound to be alert for if you are ever in the vicinity of heavy thunderstorms, or if your locality is threatened by tornadoes, is a strange hissing noise. This hissing noise, which is produced when a tornado is high in the air, has also been described as a piercing, high-pitched shriek audible for several miles. Scientists speculate that the winds inside the tornado may reach the speed of sound and thus produce the screaming, hissing noise. It may be compared to the high-pitched shriek produced by jet engines. Another possible source of the noise, especially the hissing sound, may be electrical disturbances in the cloud. Whatever the cause of the hissing sound, do not let your curiosity overwhelm you if you ever hear it. Your curiosity may cost you your life. Quickly prepare to take precautionary measures to protect yourself and others, since at any moment a tornado funnel may be upon you. The necessary precautions to protect yourself are described at the end of this chapter.

As seen from the outside, tornado funnels often look like dark upright funnels extending from the bases of heavy cumulonimbus clouds. Sometimes the funnels are very distinct; sometimes they are barely visible. They are extensions of the clouds that spawn them. They contain large amounts of condensed water vapor, dust, and debris sucked up from the ground.

Tornado funnels come in a variety of shapes, including the typical funnel or cone shape. Sometimes the funnels are inverted. At other times they are shaped like cylinders or hourglasses. Sometimes they appear as elephant trunks swinging about, or as long writhing ropes, or as long twisting pillars.

The typical funnel is about 800 to 2,000 feet long. Some funnels extend downward from the clouds and never touch the ground. Others may alternately touch the ground and rise and disappear.

Most tornado funnels are less than a mile in diameter at

their bases — the average width being about 200 to 300 yards. Some are even less than 10 feet at the tip; others are over one mile wide. Because of their relatively narrow destructive tips, the damage from tornadoes is limited to rather narrow paths along the ground. Thus, as a tornado moves through a community it may destroy blocks of houses in a row and leave adjoining blocks of houses untouched.

Tornadoes are usually accompanied by heavy downpours of rain and hail that can cause much damage. The heavy showers usually occur before or during the passage of a tornado. Very large hailstones, some as large as grapefruits, have been reported.

Movement of Tornadoes

Tornadoes have forward speeds that may range from near zero to over 70 miles per hour. Sometimes they may hover over one spot for several minutes. The typical tornado, however, usually whirls along somewhere between 20 to 40 miles per hour. Most tornadoes travel from the southwest to the northeast in advance of a strong cold front. In general, they travel from west to east. However, a very small percentage may approach from any other point on the compass. Since most tornadoes travel toward the northeast, they may be avoided by moving at right angles to their usual direction of motion. However, this evasive action could be dangerous; it should be taken only when you are trapped outdoors and no shelter is available. Since tornadoes are killers, and unpredictable, it would be wise to study the following excerpts from the bulletin *Tornado* issued by the National Oceanic and Atmospheric Administration (NOAA) of the U.S. Department of Commerce.

WHEN A TORNADO APPROACHES—YOUR IMMEDIATE ACTION MAY MEAN LIFE OR DEATH

Seek inside shelter, preferably in a tornado cellar, underground excavation, or a steel-framed or reinforced concrete building of substantial construction. STAY AWAY FROM WINDOWS!

IN CITIES OR TOWNS

In office buildings—go to an interior hallway on the lowest floor, or to the designated shelter area.

In factories—Workers should move quickly to the section of the plant offering the greatest protection in accordance with advance plans.

In shopping centers—go to a designated shelter area—not to your parked car.

In homes—the basement offers the greatest safety. Seek shelter under sturdy furniture if possible. In homes without basements, take cover in the center part of the house, on the lowest floor, in a small room such as a closet or bathroom, or under sturdy furniture. Keep some windows open, but stay away from them!

Mobile homes are particularly vulnerable to destructive winds. Proper tie-downs to prevent overturning will minimize damage. A warden should be appointed in mobile-home parks to scan the skies and listen to radio and television for warnings. There should be a designated community shelter where residents can assemble during a tornado warning. If there is no such shelter, do not stay in a mobile home during a tornado warning. Seek refuge in a sturdy building or a ditch, culvert, or ravine.

IN SCHOOLS

Whenever possible, follow advance plans to an interior hallway or the lowest floor. AVOID AUDITORIUMS and GYMNASIUMS or other structures with wide free-span roofs. If a building is not of reinforced construction, go quickly to a nearby reinforced building, or a ravine or open ditch and lie flat.

IN OPEN COUNTRY

If there is no time to find suitable shelter, lie flat in the nearest depression, such as a ditch or ravine.

KEEP LISTENING

Your radio and television stations will broadcast the latest National Weather Service tornado watches and warnings, and inform you when the danger is over.

WATCH THE SKY

Tornadoes come and go so quickly there may not be time for a warning. During a tornado watch, be alert for the sudden appearance of violent wind, rain, hail, or funnel-shaped cloud. When in doubt, take cover. Tornadoes are often obscured by rain or dust. Some occur at night.

REMEMBER:

TORNADO WATCH

means tornadoes are expected to develop.

TORNADO WARNING

means a tornado has actually been spotted. Persons close to the storm should take cover immediately. Those farther away should take cover if threatening conditions approach.

VII

Hurricanes

August 18, 1973: Brenda, a tropical storm, sprang to life this day in the Caribbean, and for the first time in history the birth of a hurricane was viewed by the human eye from a vantage point off the earth. High above the Caribbean, in space, astronauts aboard Skylab saw the circular wind-streaked cloud pattern of Brenda in its developing stages. They radioed back to earth, "It looks like it's just being born out there — you can see the circular pattern of an embryonic tropical storm. We'll try to keep an eye on it for you. . . ."

As the astronauts beamed television pictures of Brenda back to earth, the National Weather Service's hurricane warning centers mobilized their forces to investigate the disturbance and track its movement. Before Brenda was identified as a tropical disturbance, a steady flow of weather data from ships, aircraft, and weather stations was routinely transmitted to the National Meteorological Center near Washington, D.C. The assembled data were analyzed and then transmitted as facsimile maps to weather stations throughout the United States and overseas. At Suitland, Md., the National Environmental Satellite Service received photographs of cloud cover transmitted by orbiting satellites. These photographs were modified by the addition of geographic coordinates and landforms and then transmitted to weather stations. And at Miami and Puerto Rico, photographs were also received when a weather satellite was within range. With such data readily available, weather forecasters search for atmospheric processes that indicate the beginnings of a hurricane. Among the things they watch for are changes in clouds, steady rainfall, intensified winds, and below-normal atmospheric pressure. When the forecasters believe that a tropical storm is developing, reconnaissance aircraft are dispatched to the area to make a thorough investigation.

When aerial reconnaissance confirms the development of a disturbance into a tropical storm, a hurricane emergency begins — and the hurricane warning system moves into action.

Hurricanes in the New World

Probably the earliest encounter with a hurricane in the Americas was recorded by Christopher Columbus. Some historians believe he encountered a hurricane in the vicinity of Santo Domingo in 1494 and again in 1495. Fortunately, no hurricanes lashed Columbus' ships in 1492 when they sailed into the New World. The only encounter recorded by Columbus that may have been associated with a hurricane occurred when high seas bounced his little ships about. The *Niña, Pinta,* and *Santa Maria* were probably being bounced about by waves driven away from a distant hurricane. Although you may have read elsewhere that the *Santa Maria* was wrecked on a reef, it was not this encounter with rough seas that resulted in its destruction. The *Santa Maria* was wrecked later in the year during a winter storm.

Several years later, in December 1503, Columbus recorded an encounter with a storm in the Caribbean that from its description sounds like a true hurricane. He recorded: "the wind . . . prevented our progress . . . we were forced to keep out in this bloody ocean . . . lightning broke forth . . . water never ceased to fall from the sky."

After Columbus, numerous Spanish explorers also sailed to the New World, and several of them encountered hurricanes. Throughout the Caribbean the explorers found that the Indians had a number of names for hurricanes that were quite similar. Names such as Hunraken—the Mayan storm god; Hurakan—the Quiche god of thunder and lightning, and other similar sounding names for big wind and evil spirit led the Spanish explorers to call these tropical tempests *huracan*. From this word, hurricane was derived by the English.

As the early explorers plied their way back and forth from the Caribbean to Europe, sporadic hurricanes took their toll of ships and men. In 1502 one fleet of twenty ships, with their holds loaded with tons of gold, was virtually destroyed by a hurricane in the waters between Puerto Rico and Hispaniola. Only one ship stayed afloat. To this day, the remainder with their gold-laden hulls lie on the ocean floor in water about 1,800 feet deep. Other ships, also loaded with treasure, have been sunk in much shallower water. Such ships are regularly being searched for by treasure hunters throughout the Caribbean region.

Forces at Work Within Hurricanes

Although numerous ships have been sent to watery graves during hurricanes, the most death and destruction caused by these storms occurs on islands, along coasts, and even inland on the continents. The greatest amount of death and damage is caused by powerful winds that hammer away at trees, power lines, and buildings, and produce huge sea waves and masses of piled-up water (storm surge), which inundate coastal areas. In addition, in inland areas heavy rains often cause serious flooding.

Winds within hurricanes range from a low of 74 miles per hour to over 200 miles per hour. As winds increase, the pressures produced by the winds increase dramatically. For example, a 60-mile-per-hour wind may exert a pressure of 15 pounds per square foot; a 150-mile-per-hour wind may exert a pressure of 112 pounds per square foot.

According to engineers, some damage to structures occurs when wind pressures reach about 15 to 20 pounds per square foot. Buildings that are properly designed and constructed suffer slight damage as compared to flimsy buildings, which may be demolished. However, a pressure of 20 pounds per square foot represents the force exerted by winds in the lowest range of hurricane wind speeds. The death and destruction wrought by winds in the general range of 125 to 200 miles per hour is devastating. For example, in 1926 a hurricane with wind speeds of about 100 to 130 miles per hour struck Florida. Various eyewitness accounts of the hurricane indicate the savage fury of the storm. Telephone poles and trees were knocked over like matchsticks. Rooftops, frame and all, were torn loose and thrown down streets like women's hats blown off on a blustery March day. At times entire blocks of homes collapsed—loose materials such as lumber, furnishings, even people were thrown about violently. Torn timbers, roof fragments, and other objects tumbling and spinning through the air at great speeds became deadly missiles. One man was beheaded by a flying piece of iron.

In addition to the destruction caused by powerful winds hammering away, tidal waves and floodwaters surged through coastal regions, thus compounding the tragedy. When the storm subsided, after about two days, 25,000 people in Miami alone were without shelter.

A more tragic instance of a devastating hurricane occurred in Galveston, Texas, at the turn of the century. In September of 1900, a killer storm howling across the Gulf of Mexico lashed into Galveston, a coastal city. The violence that followed is unbelievable. As the winds howled, water rose rapidly along the waterfront section where thousands of people lived. Much of the city was less than ten feet above sea level; the highest land was only about fifteen feet above sea level. As the waters rose rapidly, thousands of people became trapped by the churning waters. Those who could travel toward higher ground were often injured or killed by slate shingles driven by powerful hundred-plus-miles-per-hour winds. Thousands of slate shingles flew through the air, since the fire laws of Galveston made it illegal to use flammable wooden shingles on rooftops. Eventually, the rising storm tide virtually inundated the entire city. Whole homes, remnants of homes, huge timbers, and trees floated about. Driven by the wind and powerful currents of swirling water, the assorted debris slammed against partially flooded homes, causing them to disintegrate. In the harbor, numerous houses floated about amid drifting ships that had torn loose from their anchor moorings.

As the storm subsided, the piled-up waters rushed back to the sea, often with greater speed than they had arrived. These outrushing waters added to the destruction of the city and took a great many lives.

When the waters had finally receded, thousands of bodies —humans, horses, pets, cows—lay motionless in mud and slime. About half of Galveston had been totally destroyed; the remainder of the city was virtually uninhabitable. It is estimated that 6,000 humans lost their lives. The exact number of lives taken could not be determined, since whole families were wiped out and numerous vacationers were in town at the time.

The survivors of the storm had to make an important decision: move, or stay and rebuild the city. Those who remained not only rebuilt the city but also built a huge sea-wall to keep out hurricane-driven seas. In addition, the entire city was elevated 10 to 17 feet by hauling sand into the area.

Since Galveston, the devastation caused by hurricanes has continued unabated throughout this century. Some of the most destructive hurricanes to strike the continental United States are listed below:

SOME HURRICANE DISASTERS — 1900 TO 1972

Year and Name[1]	Highest Wind Speed Recorded (land station)	Region Most Affected	Deaths	Comments
1900	120	Galveston	6,000	Half of the city destroyed
1915	106	Middle Gulf Coast	275	South of New Orleans, 90 percent of buildings destroyed
1926	132	Florida and Alabama	243	Heavy damage in Miami area and southern Alabama
1928	75	Lake Okeechobee	1,836	Lake Okeechobee overflowed into populated areas containing some large homes and hotels, but mostly small homes, shacks, and sheds of tenant farmers and sharecroppers
1938	121 and 183	Long Island, N.Y., and southern New England	600	Heavy wind and storm surge damage — New England and Long Island

Year and Name[1]	Highest Wind Speed Recorded (land station)	Region Most Affected	Deaths	Comments
1954	3 hurricanes Carol, Edna, Hazel, 100–125	Most of East Coast	176	Heavy wind damage and flooding
1955	3 hurricanes, Connie, Diane, Ione, 75–107	North Carolina to New England	216	Severe flooding in New England caused by heavy rainfall—6 to 12 inches—less than one week apart (Connie and Diane)
1957	Audrey, 100	Texas to Alabama	390	Storm surge carried water 25 miles inland in some places. Many homes destroyed; offshore oil installations damaged heavily
1969	Camille, 150–175	Mississippi, Louisiana, Alabama, Virginia, West Virginia	255 dead, 68 missing	Storm tide about 24 feet above sea level. Heavy rains —27 inches in 8 hrs; severe flash floods
1972	Agnes, 56	Florida to New York	122	One of the costliest natural disasters ever recorded—$3.5 billion. Heavy floods; 17 tornadoes

[1] Names officially adopted in 1953.

The loss of lives taken by hurricanes in other parts of the world is far greater than that suffered in the United States. The names given to counterparts of the Atlantic hurricanes are: in the Pacific, typhoons; in the Indian Ocean, cyclones. Some of the most tragic death tolls of these storms were as follows: 1737: Calcutta—300,000; 1864: Calcutta—50,000; 1881: Indochina—300,000; 1882: Bombay—100,000; 1970: East Pakistan (now Bangladesh)—200,000 (unofficial estimates as high as 500,000).

When we read of the destruction and the great loss of life taken by hurricanes we may wonder: Why are hurricanes given girls' names? How are they born? What determines their intensity and the paths they follow? The first question is the easiest to answer; for the others, scientists have some answers, but there is still much mystery about the nature of hurricanes.

Naming Hurricanes

When a tropical disturbance intensifies into a hurricane, forecasters begin to call the storm "she." During World II, tropical cyclones were given letters such as A-1943, and names such as Able, Baker, Charlie. The Air Force and Navy commonly gave them girls' names. Perhaps the novel *Storm* by G. R. Stewart (1941) inspired the use of girls' names for storms. Whatever the origin, girls' names have been used officially since 1953.

The official names assigned to tropical cyclones are shown in Table I. Names beginning with Q, U, X, Y, and Z are not included because of their scarcity. A separate list of names is used each year. Different lists are used in the Pacific. Since the average number of hurricanes in one year is about five—the record number is 21—each list should suffice for any hurricane season.

TABLE I

Tropical Cyclone Names—Atlantic, Caribbean, and Gulf of Mexico

1971	1972	1973	1974	1975	1976	1977	1978	1979	1980
Arlene	Agnes	Alice	Alma	Amy	Anna	Anita	Amelia	Angie	Abby
Beth	Betty	Brenda	Becky	Blanche	Belle	Babe	Bess	Barbara	Bertha
Chloe	Carrie	Christine	Carmen	Caroline	Candice	Clara	Cora	Cindy	Candy
Doria	Dawn	Delia	Dolly	Doris	Dottie	Dorothy	Debra	Dot	Dinah
Edith	Edna	Ellen	Elaine	Eloise	Emmy	Evelyn	Ella	Eve	Elsie
Fern	Felice	Fran	Fifi	Faye	Frances	Frieda	Flossie	Franny	Felicia
Ginger	Gerda	Gilda	Gertrude	Gladys	Gloria	Grace	Greta	Gwyn	Georgia
Heidi	Harriet	Helen	Hester	Hallie	Holly	Hannah	Hope	Hedda	Hedy
Irene	Ilene	Imogene	Ivy	Ingrid	Inga	Ida	Irma	Iris	Isabel
Janice	Jane	Joy	Justine	Julia	Jill	Jodie	Juliet	Judy	June
Kristy	Kara	Kate	Kathy	Kitty	Kay	Kristina	Kendra	Karen	Kim
Laura	Lucille	Loretta	Linda	Lilly	Lilias	Lois	Louise	Lana	Lucy
Margo	Mae	Madge	Marsha	Mabel	Maria	Mary	Martha	Molly	Millie
Nona	Nadine	Nancy	Nelly	Niki	Nola	Nora	Noreen	Nita	Nina
Orchid	Odette	Ona	Olga	Opal	Orpha	Odel	Ora	Ophelia	Olive
Portia	Polly	Patsy	Pearl	Peggy	Pamela	Penny	Paula	Patty	Phyllis
Rachel	Rita	Rose	Roxanne	Ruby	Ruth	Raquel	Rosalie	Roberta	Rosie
Sandra	Sarah	Sally	Sabrina	Sheila	Shirley	Sophia	Susan	Sherry	Suzy
Terese	Tina	Tam	Thelma	Tilda	Trixie	Trudy	Tanya	Tess	Theda
Verna	Velma	Vera	Viola	Vicky	Vilda	Virginia	Vanessa	Vesta	Violet
Wallis	Wendy	Wilda	Wilma	Winnie	Wynne	Willene	Wanda	Wenda	Willette

Birth of a Hurricane

Before a hurricane is named, of course, it has to be born. And the birth of a hurricane is not exactly understood. Often, when it appears that the conditions necessary for the birth of a hurricane have developed inside an ordinary tropical storm, the disturbance may weaken and dissipate. At other times the myriad atmospheric conditions favorable for hurricane development are in delicate balance and the hurricane mechanism is triggered.

The atmospheric conditions necessary for the development of a hurricane are found principally in the regions encompassing the Caribbean and the Gulf of Mexico, the Bahamas southeastward to the Lesser Antilles, and further eastward to the Cape Verde Islands off the west coast of Africa. Early in the hurricane season—May and June—the principal areas of origin are the Caribbean and the Gulf of Mexico. As the season progresses, the principal source region shifts eastward across the Atlantic until about mid-September, when it lies in the region of the Cape Verde Islands. After mid-September the shift is back to the Caribbean and the Gulf of Mexico. By mid-October, the threat of hurricanes is sharply diminished; by November, the hurricane season is essentially ended. As shown in Fig. 1, the months at the beginning and end of the hurricane season—May, June and October, November—have relatively few hurricanes; the peak of the hurricane season is in the latter part of the summer.

The atmospheric setting for the growth of a hurricane is a large expanse of the atmosphere resting upon the warm waters of a tropical ocean. The region most conducive to hurricane development is located largely between the equator and the Tropic of Cancer. Within this region the easterly trade winds of the Northern and Southern hemispheres converge in a low-pressure trough located between the Azores — Bermuda high of the North Atlantic and its high-pressure counterpart in the South Atlantic. This zone of low pressure,

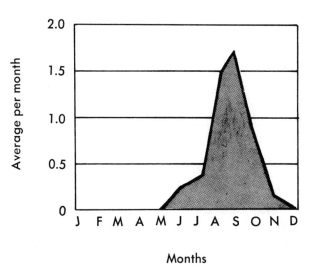

Hurricane Average Per Month

North Atlantic Ocean

1886–1966

Months

FIG. 1

you may recall, is commonly referred to as the doldrums. It is also more exactly termed the equatorial trough or inter-tropical convergence zone.

Over this region during the warm months, sinking air from the highs (anticyclones) is heated by compression and decreases in relative humidity. This sinking air creates a zone of warm, relatively dry air beneath which air sweeping across the surface of warm ocean becomes laden with moisture. Convective processes within the lower level of warm, moist air produce cumuliform convective clouds that extend upward to the relatively dry air above. The dry air tends to act as a cap limiting the heights of the convective clouds to about 6,000 to 10,000 feet. Significant, even heavy rainfall of short duration is produced by these clouds. Heat energy released by condensation of cloud particles into raindrops is transported to higher levels. The easterly flow may then be sufficiently disturbed for rainstorms to become concentrated and develop into a storm system. Since a newly developed storm may be the embryo of a hurricane, forecasters watch for unusual rainfall associated with the formation of the disturbance. In addition, cloud structure and rainfall distribution are studied, because these give good clues as to whether or not the disturbance will develop into a hurricane.

The Easterly Wave and Hurricane Formation

Within the easterlies, a westward-moving trough of low pressure—the easterly wave—causes convergence and divergence of airflow. The diverging (outward-moving) air, which is associated with sinking air, produces fair to good weather. But the converging (inward-moving) air, which is associated with rising air, causes the moist layer to deepen—as a result, cumuliform clouds build up to heights of 30,000 to 40,000 feet. Thus, showers and thunderstorms accompany the easterly wave.

Throughout the summer months, a steady succession of easterly waves passes through the Caribbean. Ordinarily, these waves may travel thousands of miles with little change in their wavelike shape. Within these systems, winds ahead

of the wave are generally from the northeast. Behind the
wave (the eastern portion) winds are generally from the
southeast. If the wave can be made to curl in on itself, air
within the disturbance may ascend more rapidly. Then the
entire system can become a whirling mass that may accelerate
and attain hurricane intensity (Fig. 2).

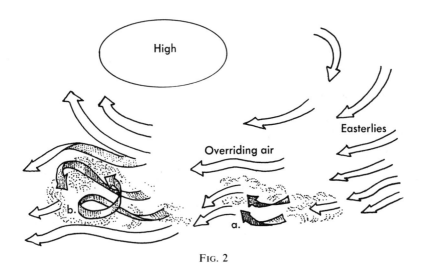

FIG. 2

Another condition that may give rise to a hurricane is the
movement of a polar trough below the Tropic of Cancer and
into the ITC, or intertropical convergence, zone. A portion
of the polar trough may become separated from the main
trough and become an easterly wave. Since polar troughs
penetrate the tropics largely in the colder seasons, they are
most likely to act as hurricane-triggering mechanisms at the
beginning and end of the hurricane season.

Weathermen know that hurricanes may originate in the

intertropical convergence zone, or the easterly waves, or as part of polar troughs. Still there is much mystery about the delicate hurricane-forming mechanism, which at times seems to be in the proper balance to build a hurricane and then sputters harmlessly, yet at other times does generate a deadly hurricane.

Within the delicate hurricane mechanism scientists have observed that ocean waters of 79° F. and higher are usually needed to spawn hurricanes. At these temperatures, found in tropical regions, the warm ocean loses relatively large quantities of water to the atmosphere by evaporation. Scientists have also noted that hurricanes do not develop at the equator, although the storms from which they are generated may have formed at the equator. The principal region of formation lies about 5° to 20° north of the equator. In the Atlantic, no storms originate south of the equator. Nor does the eastern portion of the Pacific south of the equator spawn hurricanes. The South Atlantic and the eastern section of the South Pacific probably do not generate hurricanes because water temperatures are slightly lower and the intertropical convergence zone moves only slightly below the equator during summer in the Southern Hemisphere.

According to many scientists, the Coriolis force produced by the rotating earth may contribute to the formation of hurricanes by adding the necessary spin to a tropical disturbance that will cause it to intensify and form a hurricane. This belief is supported by the fact that hurricanes do not form at the equator where the Coriolis force is zero.

The Anatomy of a Hurricane

A hurricane may be viewed as a colossal atmospheric heat engine that must be continuously fed warm, moist air to keep it going. In an incipient hurricane, moist air surrounding the storm is pumped in toward the center of the whirling mass, which is like a huge chimney many miles wide and thousands of feet high. Moisture carried upward in the chimney condenses and liberates latent heat to the core of the storm. The added heat intensifies the upsurging currents within the chimneylike core, thus reducing the air pressure within the core.

If the storm is to continue to develop, the upsurging air must have an outlet, otherwise the core will tend to fill and the pressure difference between the center of the storm and the fringes will tend to decrease. The effect would be somewhat like a vacuum cleaner in which the collecting bag has filled up. At such times, the vacuum has little "sucking-in" ability. Actually, the sucking in of dirt is caused by high-pressure air outside the vacuum forcing its way into the low-pressure area produced mechanically within the vacuum. Replacing the filled bag with an empty bag makes more room for the inrushing air and facilitates the outward movement of air. In a hurricane, more space for inrushing air is produced by the expelling of upward-rushing air at great heights into high-altitude winds, or into a larger anticyclonic system located on the outer fringes of the storm.

If we could dissect a fully developed storm and observe its structure, its air movements, and other components, we would note that the core of the howling storm is a relatively clear and calm region around which powerful winds revolve. This region, called the eye, ordinarily ranges from about 15 to 25 miles in diameter. Much smaller and much larger eyes are not uncommon, however. Essentially, the larger and more powerful a storm, the larger the eye. Within this region air pressures are usually below 28.50 inches (965 millibars). Normal atmospheric pressure is about 29.92

inches or 1013.2 miilibars. The record low for the United States was 26.35 inches (896 millibars) in 1935. In 1927 a record low of 26.18 inches (890 millibars) was recorded aboard a ship caught in a typhoon in the Pacific Ocean. High temperatures in the eye, about 10 to 15 degrees higher than the surrounding air, account for the extra low pressures within the eyes of hurricanes (Fig. 3).

The eye is an interesting phenomenon present only in hurricanes. When the eye passes over a region, there is a lull in the storm and the inexperienced tend to think the storm has ended. People who have moved to higher ground may start the trek back to their homes. Depending upon the size of the eye and the speed of the storm, the lull may last from a few minutes to several hours. In time, however, the skies rapidly darken and the second half of the storm with its howling winds moves into the area that had been relatively calm and clear a few minutes earlier. At such times, people caught outdoors may be killed or injured. For example, such an occurrence took place during the hurricane that struck Miami, Florida, in 1926. When the eye of this powerful hurricane passed over the Miami area, people thought the storm was over. They went outdoors and roamed about surveying the spectacle of death and destruction about them. Despite warnings, most people remained outdoors; before long the storm rapidly bore down upon them. Meanwhile, numerous automobiles and horse-drawn vehicles loaded with people were heading back to Miami along the causeway that connects it to the mainland. As they traversed this near-sea-level roadway a tidal wave surged toward them across the bay and engulfed them.

One of the strangest spectacles associated with the eye of a hurricane is the sight of large numbers of birds attempting to ride out the storm in the safety of the eye. Since the birds

Fig. 3 *Hurricane Debbie, large eye clearly visible, is seen from ESSA 9 satellite at 2 P.M on August 19, 1969.*

cannot fly out of the eye they must travel with the storm. Thus, the eye often contains an assortment of birds unfamiliar to observers on the ground. At times, tropical birds have ended up in New England—more than 2,000 miles from their normal habitat.

Hurricane Clouds and Winds

Enclosing the eye are towering walls of clouds in which the heaviest rains fall and the strongest winds occur. The bases of these clouds are generally 500 feet above the ground; they extend upward 40,000 to 50,000 feet. These heavy clouds, spiraling skyward as thick bands of cumulus and cumulonimbus clouds, build upward to the convective level, where they spread out and form strands and sheets of cirrus clouds. Within the huge clouds, thunderstorm activity is observed. In the forward and outer section of an advancing hurricane, relatively weak tornadoes may be spawned.

The clouds and winds associated with hurricanes ordinarily extend outward about 100 to 450 miles from the eye. At the outer fringes of the storm, rains are light and winds are in the neighborhood of 30 to 40 miles per hour. As one moves toward the eye, varying amounts of rainfall will be observed and winds will steadily increase. Within about 30 miles from the eye of a storm the strongest winds—usually from 100 to 150 miles per hour—are encountered. In some instances, winds have been estimated at more than 200 miles per hour. In a typical storm, the strongest winds are found in the sector to the right of the storm's direction of motion. When a storm reaches its peak and begins to die out, the strongest winds may be found far from the eye.

Movement of Hurricanes

Although wind speeds within the swirling vortex of a hurricane are over 74 miles per hour, the swirling mass itself may move at about 10 to 30 miles per hour. The movements of the storm are analogous to a rapidly spinning top slowly drifting across a floor. In the earlier stages of development, slow movement—less than 20 miles per hour—results in intensification of the storm. Also, when the storm is fully developed, greater movement often results in intensification. As the typical hurricane matures it curves toward higher latitudes and accelerates to about 20 to 30 miles per hour. Occasionally, hurricanes attain forward speeds of 60 miles per hour.

The path hurricanes follow once they develop is largely westward from their source region. Eventually, they tend to move northward into the region of the prevailing westerlies, which tend to curve them north and eastward. The typical path is parabolic, that is, somewhat like a U lying on its side with its open end facing the right. Although the typical hurricane tends to follow a parabolic path, there are numerous exceptions. Some storms zigzag, some reverse direction, others form loops, or follow other erratic paths.

Although scientists cannot fully explain the erratic paths taken by hurricanes, they have noticed that wind and pressure systems play an important part in determining their direction of movement. For example, the prevailing westerlies cause them to reverse their westerly paths. Also, high-altitude winds seem to have a steering effect on storms. And high-pressure systems act as barriers, whereas low-pressure systems tend to attract them.

Death of a Hurricane

Once a hurricane curves northward it moves into regions that cannot supply the heat and moisture it needs to thrive. At higher latitudes air pulled into the system is cooler than the air at lower latitudes. And evaporation of moisture from the ocean decreases as the storm moves farther north. Very slowly, then, a northward-moving hurricane becomes deprived of the "fuel" it needs to sustain its huge heat engine. If a storm moves over land, it decays more rapidly, since it does not have the ocean waters to sustain it and it encounters greater resistance so that frictional drag increases. Eventually, the storm diminishes in intensity, winds die down, and the storm becomes much like the typical cyclonic disturbances (lows) of middle latitudes. However, rains associated with the hurricane may continue and cause flooding in inland areas. One of the most disastrous floods occurred in August of 1955 when hurricane Connie dumped 6 to 12 inches of rain over the region extending from North Carolina to New England. This unusually heavy rainfall saturated the ground and filled the rivers and lakes throughout the region. Only a few days later, Diane moved through the same region. Although Diane's winds dropped below hurricane force, heavy rains continued. As the storm moved northward, the new rainfall ran off the previously soaked ground and caused the already filled streams to overflow their banks. The resulting flood damage was so great that Diane earned the title of "the billion-dollar hurricane." In addition, about 200 people lost their lives — largely by drowning (Fig. 4).

Taming Hurricanes

Since a typical hurricane may in one day release the equivalent energy of hundreds of 20-megaton hydrogen (fusion) bombs, or have the equivalent energy of the total electrical energy produced in the United States over a six-month period, controlling hurricanes may seem to be an insurmountable problem. Yet, under Project Stormfury, scientists have undertaken the task of conducting experiments designed to take the punch out of hurricanes.

In this project, scientists have conducted cloud-seeding experiments that involved using aircraft to release silver iodide particles into hurricane clouds. It is believed that the seed particles cause supercooled cloud droplets to change to ice. Heat is released by this process. This additional heat

FIG. 4   *Hurricane damage Fire Island, N.Y. 1962.*

steps up cloud growth, which results in condensation of water vapor that supplies additional heat to the clouds. Thus, temperatures outside the eye increase, causing pressures between the eye and the region surrounding it to become more equalized. With pressure differences being lessened it is believed that the strong winds will diminish. In actual experiments on hurricanes in the early 1960's scientists found, in one storm, that part of the eyewall was modified; in another experiment the pressure within the eye of a storm rose. In 1969 a hurricane (Debbie) was seeded several times on two different days. Winds diminished on both seeding days, indicating that seeding may be an effective method of modifying hurricanes. However, hurricane modification and control are in the earliest stages of development. Until scientists learn to tame hurricanes, it is important to know the necessary precautions one should take when a hurricane warning is issued. The following safety rules issued by the National Oceanic and Atmospheric Administration of the U.S. Department of Commerce will help save your life and the lives of others if you are ever threatened by a hurricane.

HURRICANE SAFETY RULES

Hurricane advisories will help you save your life . . . but you must help. Follow these safety rules during hurricane emergencies:

(1) **Enter each hurricane season prepared.** Every June through November, recheck your supply of boards, tools, batteries, nonperishable foods, and the other equipment you will need when a hurricane strikes your town.

(2) **When you hear the first tropical cyclone advisory,** listen

for future messages; this will prepare you for a hurricane emergency well in advance of the issuance of watches and warnings.

(3) **When your area is covered by a hurricane watch,** continue normal activities, but stay tuned to radio or television for all National Weather Service advisories. Remember, a hurricane watch means possible danger within 24 hours; if the danger materializes, a hurricane warning will be issued. Meanwhile, keep alert. Ignore rumors.

(4) **When your area receives a hurricane warning: Plan your time** before the storm arrives and avoid the last-minute hurry, which might leave you marooned, or unprepared.

Keep calm until the emergency has ended.

Leave low-lying areas that may be swept by high tides or storm waves.

Leave mobile homes for more substantial shelter. They are particularly vulnerable to overturning during strong winds. Damage can be minimized by securing mobile homes with heavy cables anchored in concrete footing.

Moor your boat securely before the storm arrives, or evacuate it to a designated safe area. When your boat is moored, leave it, and do not return once the wind and waves are up.

Board up windows or protect them with storm shutters or tape. Danger to small windows is mainly from wind-driven debris. Larger windows may be broken by wind pressure.

Secure outdoor objects that might be blown away or up-rooted. Garbage cans, garden tools, toys, signs, porch furniture, and a number of other harmless items become missiles of destruction in hurricane winds. Anchor them or store them inside before the storm strikes.

Store drinking water in clean bathtubs, jugs, bottles, and cooking utensils; your town's water supply may be contaminated by flooding or damaged by hurricane floods.

Check your battery-powered equipment. Your radio may be your only link with the world outside the hurricane, and emergency cooking facilities, lights, and flashlights will be essential if utilities are interrupted.

Keep your car fueled. Service stations may be inoperable for several days after the storm strikes, because of flooding or interrupted electrical power.

Stay at home, if it is sturdy and on high ground; if it is not, move to a designated shelter, and stay there until the storm is over.

Remain indoors during the hurricane. Travel is extremely dangerous when winds and tides are whipping through your area.

Monitor the storm's position through National Weather Service advisories.

Beware the Eye of the Hurricane

If the calm storm center passes directly overhead, there will be a lull in the wind lasting from a few minutes to half an hour or more. Stay in a safe place unless emergency repairs are absolutely necessary. But remember, at the other side of the eye, the winds rise very rapidly to hurricane force, and come from the opposite direction.

---

(5) **When the hurricane has passed:**

Seek necessary medical care at Red Cross disaster stations or hospitals.

Stay out of disaster areas. Unless you are qualified to help, your presence might hamper first-aid and rescue work.

Drive carefully along debris-filled streets. Roads may be undermined and may collapse under the weight of a car. Slides along cuts are also a hazard.

Avoid loose or dangling wires, and report them immediately to your power company or the nearest law enforcement officer.

Report broken sewer or water mains to the water department.

Prevent fires. Lowered water pressure may make fire fighting difficult.

Check refrigerated food for spoilage if power has been off during the storm.

Remember that hurricanes moving inland can cause severe flooding. Stay away from river banks and streams.

Tornadoes spawned by hurricanes are among the storms' worst killers. When a hurricane approaches, listen for tornado watches and warnings. A tornado watch means tornadoes are expected to develop. A tornado warning means a tornado has actually been sighted. When your area receives a tornado warning, seek inside shelter immediately, preferably below ground level. If a tornado catches you outside, move away

from its path at a right angle. If there is no time to escape, lie flat in the nearest depression, such as a ditch or ravine.

HURRICANE WATCHES MEAN A HURRICANE MAY THREATEN AN AREA WITHIN 24 HOURS.

HURRICANE WARNINGS MEAN A HURRICANE IS EXPECTED TO STRIKE AN AREA WITHIN 24 HOURS.

Bibliography

Battan, Louis J. *The Nature of Violent Storms.* New York: Anchor Books – Doubleday and Co., 1961.

Bell, Corydon. *Wonder of Snow.* New York: Hill and Wang, 1957.

Chapelle, Edward R. *Field Guide to Snow Crystals.* Seattle: University of Washington Press, 1969.

Clausse, Roger, and Facy, Leopold. *The Clouds.* New York: Evergreen Profile Book – Grove Press, Inc., 1961.

Dunn, G. E., and Miller, B. I. *Atlantic Hurricanes.* Baton Rouge, La.: Louisiana State University Press, rev. ed., 1964.

Edinger, James G. *Watching for the Wind.* New York: Anchor Books – Doubleday and Co., 1967.

Harris, Miles F. *Opportunities in Meteorology.* New York: Vocational Guidance Manuals, 1972.

Lane, Frank W. *The Elements Rage.* Philadelphia: Chilton Co., 1965.

Lehr, Paul E., Burnett, R. Will, and Zim, Herbert S. *Weather: Air Masses, Clouds, Rainfall, Storms, Weather Maps, Climate.* New York: Simon and Schuster, 1957.

Milgrom, Harry. *Understanding Weather.* New York: Crowell-Collier Press (Macmillan), 1970.

Tufty, Barbara. *1001 Questions Answered about Storms and Other Natural Disasters.* New York: Dodd Mead, 1970.

World Meteorological Organization. *How to Become a Meteorologist,* 1970.